The Meltin' Pot

A combination of flavors from different cultures around the world.

50+ creative recipes accompanied by stunning photos that utilize simple ingredients to give your cooking a new spin!

Carolyn Hoyte

Copyright © 2021 by Carolyn Hoyte. All rights reserved. No part of this publication may be reproduced, distributed, or transmitted in any form or by any means, including photocopying, recording, or other electronic or mechanical methods, without the prior written permission of the author, except in the case of brief quotations embodied in critical reviews and certain other non-commercial uses permitted by copyright law.

For more information please contact:

Carolyn Hoyte
404-969-6701
info@carolynhoyte.com
www.carolynhoyte.com

Photo Credits: Carolyn Hoyte, Victor Brown's Photography, Unsplash (Prop staging)

Layout and design: Dionne Jones (www.dijotalmedia.com)
www.dijotalmedia.com

Published by: Carolyn Hoyte

ISBN: 979-8-9851524-0-1

To my Dad

I dedicate this book to my Dad, my hero, a man of singular integrity and honor. Until the day he died, my Dad made me feel protected and loved. My father was a great man. He was loving, kind, honest and hard-working. The way he lived his life exemplified all these qualities. I started this book years ago but kept procrastinating. When my Dad passed away last year, I knew, I had to finish it, in honor of him.

I have included in this book, some of my Dad's favorite dishes, that I often cooked for him and my Mom. I will always love my Dad and will never forget him. I miss his smile, his dancing feet, his steady demeanor. His face is forever etched in my memory and the essence of him runs through my veins, enabling me to be the person I am today. I have been fortunate to marry a man who possesses many of the qualities of my Dad, and each day, I am reminded of this, in our interactions.

My uncle told me, "always remember, death cannot kill what never dies." My love for my Dad lives on in me and my family.

Thank You

Many thanks to my patient and devoted supporters, you've asked and waited for many years for my book to come out and now it's finally here. You supported me with the cooking magazine we created on a whim during the pandemic last year but never abandoned the need for a great cookbook. Thank you.

To my friend Dionne Jones, who wears many hats, thank you! She is my editor, book designer, and producer from the beginning of this journey. You make me look so good. I am grateful to you.

To my biggest fan/supporter, my husband Orin Hoyte. You are constantly pushing me to get to the next level. My simple "thank you" feels like it is not enough for all the chances you take with me because of how much you believe in me. I am truly grateful and blessed to have a partner like you.

To my amazing two children, Saidah and Orin Jr. none of this would've been possible without your unwavering support. You were my photographer, my taste tester, my food critic, and most of all my two joys...I love you and thank you.

Contents

Foreword
7

Preface
8

Appetizers
9

Entrees
33

Sides
65

Salads & Salsas
79

Desserts
89

Cocktails/Drinks
103

Index
111

Glossary
112

Appendix
115

Foreword

"When I entered culinary school I wanted to get the best experience possible because this was going to be the foundation to my career. I sat at the front of all of my classes, and tried to be extremely selective in any partner that I was going to be working with. Long story short I was uptight! Sometimes life gives you what you need, regardless if you know that's what you want. Carolyn and I were paired together in one class, and I have admired her skill many years later, just as I did that night. Chef Carolyn Hoyte proved to be the best person to work with then and now! Where I over thought, and stumbled to find my own style in the beginning of my career. Carolyn was always laser focused in her cooking, and gave a complete picture without compromise. Her food has always been delicious, but many home cooks make a delicious meal. She loves to make her meals memorable, edible art! Carolyn, was relaxed in her preparation, but impeccable in her presentation! I had taken a few pages from her book, and used them well in my own career. I have had the honor of attending events from Chef Hoyte's catering company, every element is curated to highlight her attention to detail. Center pieces, lighting, linens, and every passed Hor d'oeuvre, makes sure to emphasize her vision. Very few things have changed in her passion for a profession, which burns out many gifted culinarians.

The book that you are about to read is going to give you meals that you can use during a week night or celebratory dinner. Chef Carolyn's range is vast and her knowledge extensive. This cookbook will have your meals to the level of a professional chef without requiring the culinary school education. Carolyn's experience will be your secret weapon that is unless you choose to share this cookbook as a gift! I am so happy that she is able to share this first installment into her kitchen for everybody to experience.

I have been a Chef now for over 15 years, and have worked with many chefs through the years. I can say without any hesitation that Chef Hoyte has a unique voice in the culinary field. Many Chefs' lack the ability to share their skill, or lack the originality to inspire. After knowing Carolyn for 15 years, I feel confident that lack of originality has never been her issue. I hope you come to enjoy this book and refer to it recipes to make your own cooking inspire others!"

Chef Alex Lewis CEC, M.ED

Thank You In Advance,

Alex Lewis, M.Ed. CEC
Culinary Arts Instructor
912 443 5522
Savannah Technical College
5717 White Bluff Road
Savannah, GA 31405

Preface

melt•ing pot

/ˈmeltiNG ˌpät/
different peoples, styles, theories, etc. are mixed together.
"a melting pot of disparate rhythms and cultures"

This cookbook is a melting pot of international recipes from around the world! In The Meltin' Pot, you'll explore a wide range of cuisines as you learn to cook delicious entrees, soups, sauces, and even desserts from all over the globe.

You and your family will have a chance to experience a variety of culinary traditions as you try your hand at this diverse array of international cooking.

Each recipe is accompanied by an attractive photograph and helpful hints.

The Meltin' Pot! While the first thing that comes to mind would be cheese, when I named my book this was the furthest thing from my mind. As a chef, I love experimenting with dishes from many cultures, maybe it is the fact that I am from Guyana, home to six ethnic groups - The Indigenous Amerindian, the East Indians, Africans, Portuguese, Europeans and Chinese. Guyana is a melting pot of cultures, a culture that celebrates everything with food, I wanted to know more, I was inquisitive, and that rich culinary culture fuelled my passion.

My journey to becoming a chef started in 2008 with me being a Realtor. When the market started to decline, I was curious about taking a cooking class, so I visited the Le Cordon Bleu thinking that I have some downtime to do a little 3 months course to have some fun. To my surprise when I got there, it was a 12-month in-class course and a 3 months externship for $40K. whewww!!..I got home and sat on my stairs, my husband came out and asked "How was it" I looked at him and laughed..... that is 40k for 15 months....he was like ouch...then turned around and said " you are good at it you should do it" "I was like... what??....are you crazy? This is just a hobby". He said, "But it makes you happy, so do it". I was excited and took the plunge, now here I am. After completion, he said to me ...now go make that money...LOL

One of the recipes in my cookbook is Pepperpot, I am partial to Asian food but this is my most favorite dish to prepare. Pepperpot is the National dish of Guyana, origination from the Native people. While it can be prepared year-round, it is the cornerstone dish of Christmas celebrations, Christmas in Guyana doesn't seem quite complete without it.

In addition to some signature Guyanese dishes, I have included in my book, a taste of ethnicities from around the world, many being part of the fabric which is my heritage. So come into my kitchen and cook with me.

APPETIZERS

Appetizers

Salmon Cakes	11
Caprese Crostini	13
Charcuterie Board	15
Roasted Red Pepper Bisque	17
Bacon & Cheese Cauliflower Rice Balls w/ Sriracha Dip	19
Prosciutto Crostini with Goat Cheese & Fig Jam	21
Pineapple Jerk Chicken Wings	23
Shrimp Cerviche	25
Korean Taco	27
Crab Cakes	29
Vegetable Spring Rolls	31

Salmon Cakes

These salmon cakes come together quickly with a few ingredients, pan frying for a crispy crust, and perfect serving size. They are great as is or with your favorite dipping sauce.

Pro Tip

What to Serve with Salmon Cakes

Salmon cakes can be served with a wedge of lemon, or a dollop of tartar sauce. Complete your meal with a simple side salad or a scoop of coleslaw and warm crusty french bread

Storing and Freezing Salmon Patties

Once cooked, leftover cakes can be stored in the fridge for up to three days. Eat them cold, or warm them up in a skillet over low heat or pop them in the microwave.

Salmon cakes also freeze well. Wrap them in wax or parchment paper, plastic and foil, defrost them in the fridge before reheating.

INGREDIENTS

2 14oz cans wild salmon
2 eggs, beaten
2 cups panko bread crumbs
1/2 cup onions
1/2 cup assorted peppers (chopped)
1/4 cup celery
2 tablespoons fresh lemon juice
2 tablespoons mayonnaise
2 tablespoons scallions
1 tablespoon minced garlic
1 tablespoon Dijon mustard
2 tablespoons mayonnaise
1 tablespoon garlic salt
1/2 tablespoon cayenne
Olive oil

INSTRUCTIONS

Drain salmon then remove and discard any bones or cartilage. Transfer salmon to a medium bowl and flake into small chunks using a fork. Add egg, peppers, onions, lemon juice, mayonnaise, celery, mustard, mayo, garlic salt, and cayenne to salmon and mix until thoroughly combined. (leave the panko for coating the salmon)

Using an ice cream scoop, scoop a level amount of salmon mixture and form into a patty, about 2 1/2-inches in diameter and 1/2-inch thick. Roll in the breadcrumbs; transfer to a plate and repeat with the remaining mixture. Place in the refrigerator for 20 minutes to firm up.

Heat a nonstick skillet over medium-high. Add 3 tablespoon oil and heat just until shimmering. Place the salmon cakes in skillet and cook, without moving, until golden brown, 2–2 1/2 minutes. Carefully flip patties and cook until the second side is golden brown, 2–2 1/2 minutes. Transfer patties to a wire rack.

Wipe out the skillet with a paper towel and repeat the cooking process with the remaining tablespoon of oil and salmon patties. Serve warm and enjoy!!!

Caprese Crostini

Add a burst of flavor to your caprese with this simple and creative crostini. A beautiful appetizer with minimal ingredients will set the tone for any dinner party.

Pro Tip

The flexibility of the recipe is one of the things that makes it so great. Although my recipe calls for mozzarella, you can use any other cheese if you prefer.

Want things a little salty? Add some capers. Make the recipe your own!

INGREDIENTS

15 slices of French baguette
3- 4 Roma tomatoes
Olive oil
Sea salt and freshly ground black pepper
Sliced fresh mozzarella
Thai basil leaves

INSTRUCTIONS

Preheat oven to 350° F.

Slice the baguette and place on a baking sheet.

Brush olive oil on both sides of the baguette slices.

Bake the baguette slices for approx. 10-15 minutes or until golden brown.

Remove from the oven and allow them to cool to room temperature.

Once the baguette slices have cooled, begin to assemble.

Top with slices of tomato, fresh mozzarella cheese, and garnish with fresh chopped basil.

Drizzle with olive oil, salt and fresh black pepper.

Charcuterie Board

A fun and easy way to enjoy a variety of gourmet cured meats, chesses, fruit, vegetables on bread or crackers, also great for appetizers and cocktail parties. It's simple. It is in the perfect combination of flavors in each bite: bringing together artisanal flavor, premium meats, and robust pairings

Pro Tip

The keys to a great charcuterie board

Serve everything already sliced and grouped on one charcuterie board. Keep in mind that simple cheese boards and vintage bread or cutting boards work well too. If you don't have room for the bread and crackers, serve on the side. For a creative presentation, fold, roll, or layer sliced cured meat.

Pair with beer or wine

INGREDIENTS

A variety of cheeses: (include hard and soft cheese)

Nuts: (almonds, cashews, and pistachios)

Fruits: (Choose based on the season, but berries, oranges, figs, olives and kiwis all add a variety of color and flavor)

Dried Fruits: (Try apricots, dried lemons or oranges, freeze-dried strawberries)

Vegetables: (carrots, cucumbers, celery, snap peas)

Crackers: (pretzel sticks, gluten-free crackers)

Breads: French baguettes (sliced)

Meats: (salami, prosciutto)

Hummus, honey, Dijon mustard, olive tapenade or other dips

INSTRUCTIONS

Arrange on board or large platter: Start by placing any bowls or ramekins on the table. Plan to use them for nuts, olives, fruits, dips, etc. Avoid placing them all close together and space them out so that they are easily accessible from along the table.
Add cheese and place crackers nearby
Add meat
Add fruits and vegetables
Fill in gaps with nuts or dried berries
Keep toothpicks near the board
Use a variety of container heights and sizes to arrange items. Height adds dimension.

Roasted Red Pepper Bisque

Great for any occasion, this recipe provides the perfect balance of creaminess and flavor. Fresh roasted red peppers highlight the flavor of this homemade bisque.

Pro Tip

Storage

This soup should keep well in the refrigerator, covered, for several days, or freeze it in individual portions for later. Top with fresh garnishes just before serving.

INGREDIENTS

2 tablespoons butter
1 small onion
1 tablespoon minced garlic
1 can crushed tomato 28oz
1 whole roasted red pepper from jar chopped
2 1/2 cups of vegetable stock
1/4 cup sugar
1/4 teaspoon cayenne pepper
1 tablespoon fresh basil
1 tablespoon fresh oregano
1/2 cup of heavy cream
Salt and pepper

INSTRUCTIONS

Melt butter in a heavy sauce pan.

Add chopped garlic and onion and saute about 2 minutes.

Add crushed tomato and chopped roasted red pepper, cayenne pepper, basil oregano, sugar and vegetable stock. Mix well and cover. Let it come to a boil for 7 minutes.

Remove pan from heat and use an immersion blender and blend until really smooth. (if using a blender, let it cool for 5 minutes before pouring it into your blender to blend smoothly then pour back into the pot to finish).

Add in the heavy cream and stir well to blend.

Top with fresh basil and serve with a crusty bread or grilled cheese sandwich.

Bacon & Cheese Cauliflower Rice Balls with Sriracha Dip

Cauliflower balls are the tastiest way to enjoy cauliflower, with cheese and bacon inside, they create a delicious new treat. Make them vegetarian by substituting vegan bacon and cheese.

Pro Tip

Storing
Cauliflower balls keep nicely for about three to five days, meaning you can make these ahead, and have them for most of the week.

To Reheat
Drizzle a pan with some oil, heat them over a gentle flame for a few minutes, being sure to turn them a few times during the heating process.

INGREDIENTS

1 medium head of cauliflower cut into bite sized florets
1/2 cup shredded parmesan cheese
6 slices of cooked bacon chopped
2 oz cream cheese
1/2 tablespoon complete seasoning
1/4 cup chopped scallions
2 cups panko bread crumbs
1 cup flour
2 eggs whisked
salt to taste
Oil for frying

INSTRUCTIONS

Add cauliflower to a food processor. Pulse on high speed until near smooth. Add in parmesan cheese, bacon, cream cheese and scallions. Pulse until mixed. Taste and add salt if needed.

Using an ice cream scoop, scoop packed balls of mashed cauliflower and shape slightly so that they are mostly smooth and oblong. Freeze balls for 4 hours or longer.

Fill a deep pot with oil and heat to 350 degrees.

Place panko bread crumbs, whisked eggs and flour each in a bowl.

Remove the cauliflower balls from freezer, dip in the flour, then the eggs and then panko bread crumbs. Place on a baking sheet lined with parchment paper..

Deep fry for about 5 minutes until light golden brown.

Serve with sriracha dip (see recipe on page 28)

Prosciutto Crostini with Goat Cheese & Fig Jam

These easy to make Prosciutto Crostini with Goat Cheese and Fig Jam make a perfect appetizer or cocktail party food. Enjoy this decadent appetizer with friends on game night, for the big game, or for your next social gathering.

Pro Tip

Consider using apricot jam for this appetizer…this is a great substitute in case you cannot find fig jam.

INGREDIENTS

- 1 baguette
- 2 tablespoons olive oil
- 2 tablespoons honey
- 1/4 cup fig jam
- 10 basil leaves
- 5 oz soft goat cheese
- 4 oz prosciutto, thinly sliced

INSTRUCTIONS

Preheat oven to 350°.

Slice your baguette into 1/2" diagonal slices. Cutting on a diagonal will give you more space for toppings and looks better.

Place baguette slices on a baking sheet and either drizzle or brush olive oil on top of each one, just one side.

Bake the baguette slices for 8 minutes, until the edges are slightly crisp and the center is still soft. They will get a light brown color.

Whipping your goat cheese will make it creamy and easy to spread, rather than crumbly. Place your cheese into the bowl of a stand mixer or use a hand mixer to whip until creamy.

Spread about 1 tablespoon of goat cheese onto each slice.

Spread about 1 tablespoon of fig jam on top of the goat cheese.

Roll together 1/2 slice of prosciutto with 1 basil leaf and place it on top of the fig jam. Drizzle honey on top.

Pineapple Jerk Chicken Wings

These jerk chicken wings are simply amazing. It is flavored with the Caribbean jerk spice, a unique blend of chilies, thyme, pineapple juice and allspice that come together perfectly to create an unforgettable taste.

Pro Tip

If desired: mix a separate amount of the pineapple juice, crushed pineapple and toss wings in 1/2 of the pineapple jerk sauce.

INGREDIENTS

4lbs whole chicken wings
1 cup spicy jerk seasoning
1 cup jerk marinade
1 tablespoon fresh thyme
1 tablespoon salt
1 cup pineapple juice
1 cup crushed pineapple

INSTRUCTIONS

Place the wings in a large bowl with water, vinegar, and lemon, and soak the wings for 20 minutes. Rinse under cold water and let drain.

Place wings in a large bowl or a zip-lock bag. Combine the jerk seasoning mix, marinade, thyme salt, pineapple juice, and crushed pineapple in a large bowl…Using half the marinade for the chicken and reserve half for a dip. Combine the seasoning with the chicken thoroughly by making sure it is coated evenly all over.

Allow the seasoned chicken wings to sit at room temp for about 45 minutes or in the refrigerator overnight.

Place the remaining half of the seasoning mix in a small pot on the stovetop with medium heat. Boil for 5-7 minutes, adjust with salt and pepper if needed. Set to the side.

Preheat oven to 425F

Line a baking tray with foil, then place a rack (like a cooling rack or something similar) on the foil. Spray or brush the rack with a small amount of oil.

Place the wings on the rack in a single layer and bake for 20 minutes then flip the wings and continue baking for an additional 20 minutes.

Serve with remaining sauce as a dip.

Shrimp Ceviche

Satisfy your ceviche craving with this Latin American-inspired dish. Marinate shrimp with citrus juice and onion for bite, then "cook" it by serving cold. A perfect appetizer to kick off any meal

Pro Tip

You can experiment with other seasfood and fish to create your own signature

INGREDIENTS

3/4 lb medium shrimp, peeled, deveined and tails removed
2 limes (fresh lime juice)
2 lemons (fresh lemon juice)
2 medium roma tomatoes, diced (1 cup)
1/2 cup chopped red onion
1/4 cup chopped cilantro
1 medium jalapeno pepper
Salt and pepper, to taste
1/2 medium cucumber, peeled and diced (about 1 cup)
1 medium avocado, diced

INSTRUCTIONS

Bring a pot of water to a boil. Meanwhile, fill up a medium bowl with ice water, set aside.

Add shrimp to boiling water and let cook just until pink and opaque, about 1 minute.

Drain shrimp in a colander then transfer to ice water to cool for a few minutes. Drain well then chop shrimp into small pieces (about 1/2-inch).

In a medium non-reactive bowl (you can use the same bowl that was previously filled with ice water) combine shrimp, lime juice, lemon juice, tomatoes, onion, cilantro, jalapeno pepper and season with salt and pepper to taste.

Transfer to refrigerator and let rest 30 minutes to 1 hour. Toss in cucumber and avocado and serve (if desired you can strain off some of the juices).

It's delicious with tortilla chips or over tostada shells.

Korean Tacos

A marriage of Korean and Mexican cuisines that is as unexpected as it is delicious.

For the Kimchi

2 teaspoons sesame oil
1 cup chopped kimchi
1 teaspoon sugar

Heat sesame oil in small skillet over medium high heat. Add kimchi and sugar, and cook, stirring constantly, until caramelized and heated through, about 3-5 minutes; set aside.

For the Sriracha Mayonnaise

1/4 cup mayonnaise
1 tablespoon Sriracha
2 teaspoons freshly squeezed lime juice

In a small bowl, whisk together mayonnaise, Sriracha and lime juice; set aside.

Pro Tip

Make it vegetarian, substitute skirt steak for beans, seitan or any meatless options

INGREDIENTS

1 1/2 lb skirt steak
2 tablespoons brown sugar
2 tablespoons reduced sodium soy sauce
1 teaspoon sesame oil
1/4 teaspoon crushed red-pepper flakes
1/4 teaspoon of ground ginger
1/2 teaspoon garlic powder
1 tablespoon canola oil

INSTRUCTIONS

For the Korean Beef: In a small bowl, whisk together brown sugar, soy sauce, sesame oil, red pepper flakes and ginger and garlic powder. Add the skirt steak to marinate for 3 hours.

Heat oil in skillet over medium high heat. Add the skirt steak and cook until browned, about 3 minutes on each side. (depending on thickness)

Stir in soy sauce mixture until well combined, allowing to simmer until heated through, about 2 minutes; set aside.

For the Tacos

12 mini flour tortillas
1/4 cup diced red onion
2 tablespoons chopped fresh cilantro leaves
1/4 teaspoon sesame seeds

For the Tacos: Serve beef mixture in tortillas, topped with kimchi, red onion, cilantro and sesame seeds, drizzled with Sriracha mayonnaise.

Crab Cakes

These crab cakes are packed with fresh crab and combined with a unique combination of seasonings, breadcrumbs, and just the right amount of secret ingredients. They are then lightly pan-fried for a golden brown crust that adds the perfect texture without being too heavy. Enjoy our cakes as an appetizer with your favorite dipping sauce or as part of a delicious meal.

Pro Tip

Not a fan of Mayo? Tartar sauce can also do the trick.

INGREDIENTS

1 pound lump Crab meat
1 teaspoon Old Bay seasoning
3/4 cup of miracle whip
1 lemon freshly squeezed
1 cup panko (and extra for dusting)
1 teaspoon salt
1 teaspoon black pepper
3 tablespoons cup finely diced celery (you'll need one stalk)
2 tablespoons finely chopped fresh parsley
3 tablespoons each finely chopped red, orange and yellow bell pepper
Olive oil

INSTRUCTIONS

Line a baking sheet with parchment paper.

Combine the miracle whip, Old Bay, salt, celery, peppers, lemon juice, and parsley in a large bowl and mix well.

Add the crab meat (be sure to check the meat for any hard and sharp cartilage) and panko; gently fold mixture together until just combined, being careful not to shred the crab meat. Shape into 8 crab cakes (about ½ cup each) and dust the outside with additional panko and place on prepared baking sheet.

Cover and refrigerate for at least 1 hour.

Preheat a large nonstick pan to medium heat and coat with olive oil.

When the oil is hot, place crab cakes in the pan and cook until golden brown, about 2-3 minutes per side.

Be careful as oil may splatter.
Serve immediately with sriracha mayo sauce. (See page 28)

Vegetable Spring Rolls

Bite into these fresh vegetable spring rolls, and you will find them addictive. The crispy exterior is contrasted by the cool and mellow flavor from the peanut sauce

For Peanut Sauce

1/2 cup creamy peanut butter
1/2 cup filtered water
2 tablespoons rice vinegar
2 tablespoons soy sauce (use tamari if gluten free)
2 tablespoons maple syrup
1 teaspoon toasted sesame oil

In a mixing bowl, use a fork or whisk to mix all the ingredients together. The peanut butter will be quite stiff at the beginning, but do not worry. Just keep working it into the liquids. In a few minutes, the sauce will reach a creamy consistency.

Use the peanut sauce as a dip for appetizers, a salad dressing, or a sauce for noodles! Refrigerate any leftover peanut sauce for up to a week.

Pro Tip

Peanut Allergy?

Cashew butter or any other nut butter will be a great substitute

INGREDIENTS

12 22-cm rice paper wrappers
12 butter lettuce leaves
Red bell pepper, seeded and thinly sliced
Carrots, peeled and julienned
1/2 English cucumber, thinly sliced
1/4 head of red cabbage, sliced
Fresh basil leaves
Peanut Sauce

INSTRUCTIONS

Get your work space organized. Fill a shallow, wide bowl with warm water. Lightly wet the surface of the cutting board. Place the vegetables on plates or bowls and get them close to your workspace. Have a large plate ready so that you can lay your finished spring rolls on top.

Dip a rice paper wrapper into the bowl of water and circle the paper around so that the entire surface is moistened. Transfer the rice paper onto the wet board. Place a lettuce leaf on top of the rice paper. Then, lay the vegetables, mint, and basil on top, about 1/2 to 1 inch away from the bottom of the wrapper.

Starting from the bottom of the wrapper, start rolling everything towards the middle. Fold the left and right sides of the wrapper towards the center, and finish rolling up the spring roll. Place the spring roll onto your spare plate and repeat for the remaining spring rolls. (NOTE: If you find that the wrappers are quite stiff, let it sit on your cutting board for an extra 10 to 15 seconds to soften. Then, roll up the spring rolls.)

Serve the spring rolls with peanut sauce. The vegetable spring rolls are best consumed the day they are made.

ENTREES

Entrees

Ribeye Steak & Grilled Shrimp	35
Hoisin Beef	37
Butterflied Lemon Pepper Chicken	39
Blackeye Cook-up Rice	41
Pepperpot	43
Punjabi Lamb Curry	45
Chicken Gyros	47
Indian Rice Pilaf	49
Boiled and Fried Yuca	51
Bibimbap	53
Roasted Duck Breast	55
Mandarin Pancakes	57
Blackened Salmon	58
Mango Pico de Gallo	60
Asian Lamb Lollipops	61
Skirt Steak Plantain Tostadas	63

Ribeye Steak & Roasted Shrimp

The Ribeye steak is one of the most flavorful beef steaks you will ever try. The Ribeye is cut from the rib primal of beef and it is well marbled and incredibly tender.

Roasted Shrimp elevates it to surf and turf. Add roasted asparagus and potatoes to make this a filling dinner.

Pro Tip

Steak Doneness	Remove from Grill at this Temperature	Final Cooked Temperature
Rare	130 to 135°F	130 to 140°F
Medium Rare	140°F	145°F
Medium	155°F	160°F
Well Done	165°F	170°F

INGREDIENTS

For the Ribeye

2 15 ounce boneless ribeye steak
2 tablespoons fresh thyme, removed from sprigs
2 tablespoons extra virgin olive oil
2 tablespoons butter
2 tablespoon bbq dry rub
salt and pepper to taste

INGREDIENTS

For the Shrimp

16oz jumbo shrimp
1 tbsp sweet paprika
1 tbsp pink salt
olive oil

INSTRUCTIONS

Preheat the oven to 425° F.

Remove steak from the fridge 30 minutes before cooking, this is to bring the steak to room temperature and ensure your cooking times are more accurate. Season both sides liberally with bbq rub, salt, and pepper and set aside.

Clean and devein the shrimp and marinate with olive oil, salt, and paprika and set aside.

Place your shrimp in the preheated oven for roughly 4-5 minutes. Remove and set aside to plate.

Add the olive oil to the cast iron skillet and turn up high, allow the skillet to become hot first. Place the ribeye face down and sear undisturbed for 2 minutes. Flip the ribeye and sear for an additional 2 minutes. This will give your steak a nice seared edge.

Transfer your skillet directly to the oven. For rare, bake for 4-5 minutes. Medium rare, 5-6 minutes. Medium, 6-7 minutes. Remember, depending on the size of the steak, the more or less time it will take.

Remove skillet from oven and return to stovetop. Add the butter and thyme to the skillet and drizzle melted butter over the steak to add the flavor.

Transfer ribeye from the skillet to the plate immediately to stop the cooking temperature from rising. This is important to bring your steak to its final serving temperature.

Let your steak rest for 5 minutes before serving

Hoisin Beef

Your taste buds will come to life with this classic Chinese dish. Tender pieces of marinated beef are grilled to perfection. The result is a burst of bold Asian flavor that you just can't put down.

Pro Tip

Did you know?

The difference between hoisin sauce and oyster sauce. Although both sauces are used in Asian cuisine, hoisin sauce is a rich, reddish-brown sauce that has a sweet-salty flavor and can be used as an ingredient or dipping sauce. Oyster sauce is saltier and fishier than hoisin sauce but is also less sweet.

INGREDIENTS

3/4 cup Low Sodium Soy Sauce
1/4 cup Brown Sugar
2 tablespoons Sesame Oil
2 tablespoons Hoisin Sauce
2 cloves Garlic, minced
3 pounds Flanken Beef Short Ribs
Thyme sprigs for garnish

INSTRUCTIONS

In a bowl, combine soy sauce, brown sugar, sesame oil, hoisin sauce, and garlic. Add the short ribs and marinate for up to 2 hours or overnight in the refrigerator.

Preheat grill on high heat. Remove short ribs from refrigerator 30 minutes before grilling. Grill on high about 4-5 minutes per side until edges look caramelized.

Garnish with sprigs of thyme and serve immediately

Butterflied Lemon Pepper Chicken

This recipe produces a hearty and healthy entree that is easily prepared in your oven—With plenty of flavor from the lemon pepper and a crisp, tender finish, this lemony recipe will become a family favorite.

Pro Tip

How to butterfly a whole chicken

Stand the chicken upright on a large cutting board. Using a sharp chef knife, cut down each side of the backbone (save back bone in refrigerator or freezer to make a chicken stock)

Lay the whole chicken flat cut-side open. Using a boning or chef knife, cut through the breastbone. (or you can cut around the bone the cartilage between the bottom of the breasts) and remove it.

INGREDIENTS

1 whole Chicken 3-4lbs butterflied (*see notes)
2 tablespoons olive oil
2 tablespoons Lemon pepper
1 teaspoon black pepper
2 teaspoons pink Himalayan salt
1 tablespoon fresh thyme
1 teaspoon lavender
3 lemons (2 whole and 1 juiced)
2 tablespoons butter

INSTRUCTIONS

Preheat oven for 400F.

Clean chicken with cool water, lemon and vinegar. Drain the water and pat dry.

Mix the remaining ingredients in a small bowl and massage all over the chicken, inside the cavity and under the chicken skin
.
Preheat large skillet on stove top and place chicken in skillet, breast side up.

Roast for about 45 minutes to 1 hour, or until the skin is nicely golden brown and a thermometer inserted in chicken reads 165°F. Once done, remove the skillet from the oven and place on stove top under medium/low heat.

Add the butter and the freshly squeezed lemon juice to the hot skillet then spoon the lemony gravy formed at the bottom of the skillet over the chicken. Let the chicken rest at room temperature for about 15 minutes (resting the chicken allows the juices to be re-absorbed for a juicier bird) Carve and serve with your favorite sides.

Blackeye Peas Cook-up Rice

Cook-up rice is a traditional one-pot Guyanese rice dish that is generally made on the weekends. It is also customary to make and serve cook-up rice on New Year's Eve as it is said to bring good luck

Pro Tip

Cook-up rice can be made as a vegetarian meal. As another option use a combination of meats along with peas or beans of your choice. Fresh Garden salad and fried sweet plantains are a usual accompaniment

INGREDIENTS

3 - 15.5 oz cans blackeye peas- drained and rinsed
2 - 1.5 oz cans coconut milk
2 1/2 cups of white rice rinsed
3 pounds smoked turkey neck and tails (you can use whatever meat you prefer)
1 cup green seasoning finely chopped
(celery, onion, garlic, scallion, thick leaf thyme, fine thyme, ginger and habanero)
2 tablespoons dark soy sauce
2 tablespoons oil
8 sprigs thyme
1 tablespoon whole allspice
1 teaspoon ground all spice
Salt and pepper
5 cups of water

INSTRUCTIONS

Wash and clean meat and let drain. Wash your rice and let drain, set aside. Blend garlic, onion, celery, scallion, thyme, ginger and habanero. Marinate fresh meat with 1/2 cup of marinade and soy sauce for at least 1 hour. (if using smoked turkey no salt is needed).

Heat up your pot with oil then add the remaining marinade blend and cook for a few minutes then add your smoked turkey meat and stir to coat. Keep cooking for about 7 to 10 minutes before adding water to just cover the meat to continue cooking until fork tender.

Add the black eye peas, rice, coconut milk, allspice, thyme and 5 cups of water. Stir very well to combine, taste before adding salt and pepper. Cover and let simmer on medium for about 25 minutes then open, stir and check the consistency of the rice. TASTE your food.

As it continues to cook down the flavor gets more intense. Continue to taste the food for flavor and until it reaches your desired texture.

Pepperpot

Pepperpot is a traditional Amerindian (Native Guyanese) dish. Originally, it was prepared using wild meat. Cassareep, the main ingredient that gives Pepperpot its rich colour and flavour, is made by boiling the extracted juice of bitter cassava (yuca) with spices until it reaches a molasses-like consistency. Over time, local meats (as in the recipe) were added to suit various tastes and preferences.

Pepperpot is usually prepared before Christmas, as the flavour is enhanced with each passing day. It is usually eaten on Christmas morning with freshly baked bread.

Pro Tip

Store Pepperpot at room temperature and reheat daily as the Cassareep is a form of preservation so it does not require any refrigeration.

INGREDIENTS

2 lbs Beef shorts ribs
3 lbs cow foot
3 lbs oxtails
Lime juice or vinegar
6 cloves garlic
1 onion
1 bunch thyme
1/4 cup of celery
salt and black pepper to taste
1 cup sugar
24 oz cassareep (depending on the quality and thickness)
3 wiri wiri peppers or 1 scotch bonnet
8 cloves
3 cinnamon sticks

INSTRUCTIONS

Wash and clean meat with vinegar or lime juice and let drain.

Blend garlic, onion, celery and thyme. Marinate fresh meat with marinade, salt and pepper and 1/2 cup of cassareep for at least 8 hours to overnight.

Place all the meat and marinade in a large pot on high and steam the meats until all the liquid evaporates. Add enough water to cover the meat and boil for about 2 to 3 hours until the meat is fork tender.

Once it is tender, add in the remaining ingredients, sugar, cassareep, cloves, cinnamon sticks and pepper.
Keep boiling and adjust taste with salt and blackpepper.

Continue boiling for another 45 minutes to 1 hour until the desired color and sweetness is reached (I like mine spicy hot and a little sweet)

This is a large amount so feel free to cut this recipe in half for a small family. Enjoy!!!

Punjabi Lamb Curry

This Punjabi Lamb Curry is a delicious, authentic dish made with lamb simmered in a fragrant blend of spices in a traditional curry sauce.
Full of amazing flavor and incredibly tender, you're going to love it!

Green Seasoning Mix

2 celery sticks
1 onion
1 cup green onion
4 garlic cloves
1 inch piece ginger
1 habanero pepper
1 cup cilantro

Place all the ingredients in chopper or blender and mix thoroughly. Using half the seasoning to marinate the lamb.

Pro Tip

Serve over basmati rice or with Indian rice pilaf (see recipe on page 50) and with your choice of fresh salad

Make it vegetarian: Omit lamb and add chickpeas

INGREDIENTS

4lbs lamb (curry cut)
2 tablespoons mustard oil
3 tablespoons canola oil
2 Potatoes (peeled and cut into large chunks)
2 teaspoons coriander powder
4 tablespoons curry powder
2 teaspoons roasted geera powder
2 teaspoons amchar masala powder
2 teaspoons salt to taste
1 red chili pepper
Green seasoning mix

INSTRUCTIONS

Clean and wash the lamb meat with lemon juice and water and drain well.

Place the lamb in a large bowl adding ½ the green seasoning mix and all the spices, coriander powder, curry powder, geera, masala, mustard oil and salt and pepper.

Using your hands combine all the ingredients rubbing it into the meat then let it marinate in the refrigerator for a minimum of 4 hours.

Heat canola oil in a pressure cooker. (you can use a large pot if you don't own one)

When the oil is hot, add an additional 1 tablespoon of curry powder, 1/2 tsp masala, 1/2 tsp geera, 1/4 green seasoning mix and 1 chopped red chili pepper and fry for a few seconds.

Add the lamb pieces along with the marinade and fry for 5-6 minutes on high heat.

And potatoes and fry for another 4 minutes.

Now add 3-4 cups of water and pressure cook until mutton is done.

Remove the pressure cooker from heat and let the pressure release.

Open the lid and add back to the stove under medium heat. Taste and adjust seasoning and curry if needed.

Cook for another 4-5 minutes until the gravy is slightly thickened. Garnish with fresh cilantro.

Chicken Gyros

This version of the classic Greek street food is convenient, authentic, and even healthy! Who knew you could make a dish so simple so quickly while still maintaining all the flavor?

For the Salad

1 English cucumber, diced
2 tomatoes on the vine, diced
1/4 cup finely chopped red onion
2 tablespoons finely chopped fresh parsley
2 tablespoons olive oil
1 tablespoon fresh lemon juice
Kosher salt and black pepper, to taste

In a medium bowl, combine all ingredients. If not serving immediately, cover and refrigerate and do the same for the Tzatziki sauce. Combine and refrigerate.

For the Tzatziki Sauce

1 cup full fat plain Greek yogurt
1 English cucumber, peeled, grated, and strained really well of juices
1–2 cloves garlic, pressed
3 teaspoons. finely chopped fresh dill
2 tablespoons fresh lemon juice
3 teaspoons olive oil
1/2 teaspoon kosher salt
black pepper, to taste

Pro Tip

A warmed pita or naan gives the taste and texture of freshly made bread

INGREDIENTS

For the Chicken

2 pounds boneless, skinless, chicken thighs, cut into 2-inch chunks
1/4 cup olive oil
1 lemon, juiced and zested (about 1/4 cup juice)
4 cloves garlic, pressed
1 tablespoon dried oregano
1 1/2 teaspoon kosher salt
1/2 teaspoon black pepper, to taste

INSTRUCTIONS

In a large bowl, combine olive oil, lemon juice, zest, garlic, oregano, and salt. Season with black pepper, to taste. Add chicken to the bowl tossing to coat evenly and let marinate for 30 minutes at room temperature. (note: while the chicken marinates prepare the salad and tzatziki sauce).

Thread the chicken onto skewers. Lightly grease the grilling surface or cast iron skillet on medium heat and cook the skewers in a hot skillet for about 3 minutes per each of the 4 sides or until fully cooked through.

Remove chicken from the skewers and serve in warmed pita or naan bread with salad and tzatziki sauce.

East Indian Rice (Indian Pilaf)

Wondering what to serve side-by-side with your next chicken, beef, or pork dish? This rice pilaf combines aromatic savory spices and rice to create an excellent complement to any meal.

Pro Tip

Soaking rice speeds up the cooking by kick-starting the absorption of water before the rice even enters the pot. When you want perfectly separate grains, rinsing removes the thin layer of starch from the surface of each grain and helps keep the rice from sticking together

INGREDIENTS

3 cups basmati rice
8 cups boiling water
1 tablespoon salt
2 teaspoons turmeric
4 cloves
1 teaspoon cardamom powder
1/2 cinnamon stick
2 onions
3 tablespoons vegetable oil
3 tablespoons butter
1 teaspoon yellow mustard seeds

INSTRUCTIONS

Rinse the rice in cold water at least three times

Place the rice in a bowl add 1/2 tsp salt and cover with cold water, let it soak for 30 minutes to an hour.

Peel and slice the onions into thin half-moons.

Heat the vegetable oil and butter in a large skillet and cook the onions over low heat until they have softened and are starting to caramelize. Add in the 1/2 teaspoon mustard seeds and stir gently.

While the onions are cooking, pour the 8 cups water into a large pan and bring to the boil. Add the salt, turmeric, cloves, cinnamon, and cardamom (if using). Stir to dissolve the salt. Add drained rice to the water and stir gently.

Bring to a simmer and cook for 10-14 minutes until the rice is soft. (there will be lots of water left in the pan).

Drain the rice, remove the whole spices, and set it to one side until the onions are finished carmalizing.

Add the drained rice into the onions mixture and gently stir to combine.

Check the seasoning and add more salt if required.

Boiled & Fried Yuca (Cassava)

If you've never tried this root vegetable, you'll find it delightfully delicious, you'll begin to wonder what took you so long to discover this healthy tuber!

Pro Tip

Great on its own, even better paired with meat or fish dishes.

Cassava can also be used in many recipes requiring mashed potatoes

INGREDIENTS

1 pound fresh or frozen yuca
1/2 cup butter
1 onion, sliced
1 cup chopped green onions
2-3 cloves of garlic, minced
Salt and pepper, to taste

INSTRUCTIONS

Bring a large pot of water to boil. Salt the water and add yuca, making sure yuca is completely covered with water. Bring to a boil again, then lower heat and continue boiling for 20-30 minutes. Yuca will begin to split and lose its opaque color.

Drain and rinse the yuca. Remove the woody, stringy centers of the yuca and discard. Cut the yuca into halves, place in a large bowl; set aside.

Place the pot back on the stove over low heat, melt the butter add onions and saute until softened but not brown, for about 5 minutes. Add the garlic and continue to saute for an additional minute; remove from heat.

Add the yuca back to the pot, stir and season to taste with salt and pepper.

Bibimbap

Bibimbap, a staple of Korean cuisine, it's the ultimate rice bowl. It can be made with all kinds of vegetables and meats, as well as egg. It's fast, easy, and doesn't require a trip to a specialty store.

This dish is versatile and forgiving and if you are a vegan or vegetarian you can also add your own spin to it.

For the Gochujang Sauce

2 to 3 tablespoons gochujang paste or (garlic chili sauce)
1 1/2 tablespoons rice vinegar
1 tablespoon sesame oil
1 tablespoon maple syrup

In a small bowl, whisk together the gochujang paste or garlic chili sauce, vinegar, sesame oil, and maple syrup.

Spoon onto bibimbap bowls, or use as a dressing for any veggie rice bowl.

Pro Tip

Cook Rice with less water - dry rice makes better bibimbap because otherwise the final mixture may come out too soggy
Balance the texture of vegetables - you can substitute other vegetables but try to have a variety of soft, chewy and even crunchy if you can

INGREDIENTS

Bowls

1/2 English cucumber, thinly sliced
1/2 teaspoon rice vinegar
1 1/4 teaspoons sesame oil, divided
1 cup fresh mung bean sprouts
1 cup shredded carrots
4 cups baby spinach
1/2 teaspoon soy sauce
2 cups cooked short grain white rice
2 fried eggs
4 ounces sauteed shitake mushrooms
1 recipe gochujang sauce
Sesame seeds
Sea salt
Kimchi, optional, for serving
Chopped scallions, optional, for serving

INSTRUCTIONS

In a small bowl, toss the cucumber slices with 1/2 teaspoon rice vinegar, 1/4 teaspoon sesame oil and a pinch of salt. Set aside.

Bring a small pot of water to a boil. Drop in the bean sprouts and cook for 1 minute. Drain and set aside.

Heat 1/2 teaspoon sesame oil in a medium skillet over medium heat. Add the carrots and a pinch of salt. Cook, stirring for 1 to 2 minutes until a little bit soft, and then remove from the pan and set aside. Heat 1/2 teaspoon more sesame oil in the skillet and add the spinach and tamari. Cook,
tossing, for 30 seconds or until just wilted. Remove from the skillet and gently squeeze out any excess water from the spinach.

Assemble the bowls with the rice, cucumber slices, bean sprouts, carrots, and spinach. Top with a fried egg or baked tofu. Add the mushrooms, if using. Sprinkle with sesame seeds and drizzle generously with the gochujang sauce.

Serve with kimchi and scallions, if desired, and the remaining gochujang sauce on the side.

Roasted Duck Breast with (Mandarin Pancakes)

Roasted Duck breast W/Mandarin pancakes
A simple recipe for duck breast filled with flavor, roasted until golden brown, sliced and topped with a variety of fresh vegetables and served with Mandarin pancakes.

Fixings

Hoisin sauce
Carrots, sliced thinly
Green onions, sliced thinly

Pro Tip

To serve:

Put your hoisin sauce in a small bowl and your sliced carrots and green onions on a small plate. Place one or two slices of meat inside the pancake, along with the carrots and green onions.
Top with sauce and enjoy!

INGREDIENTS

2 boneless duck breasts
1/4 teaspoon salt
1 teaspoon sweet cooking wine/ Mirin
1/8 teaspoon Chinese five spice powder
1 tablespoon oil

INSTRUCTIONS

Marinate the Duck

Mix the salt, wine, and five spice powder in a small bowl and massage into the duck. Leave the duck breasts skin side up on a plate uncovered and let sit in the refrigerator overnight to marinate and to let the skin dry out.

Cook the Duck and Assemble

Next, preheat the oven broiler on low heat. Heat an oven-proof pan over medium-high heat, and add 1 tablespoon of oil to coat the pan.

Sear the duck breasts, skin side down, for 4 minutes. Move them frequently so the skin crisps up and fries in the duck fat that renders out. Turn the heat down to medium if needed.

After 4-6 minutes, or when the duck skin is a bit crispy and dark golden brown, carefully drain off the duck fat and discard (or save for later application to other recipes!). Flip the duck breasts (so they are skin side up), and transfer them to the broiler for about 3 minutes.

Be careful not to burn the skin, which at this point should be a bit crispy.
Remove the duck from the broiler and let rest for 10 to 15 minutes. The duck will be cooked about medium well and will be very juicy.

Transfer to a cutting board and, using a sharp knife, cut into thin slices. Serve the duck with your Mandarin pancakes (See recipe on page 57)

Mandarin Pancakes (for Roasted Duck Breast)

These signature pancakes are small, thin crepes that are slightly chewy on the outside and soft on the inside. The pancakes are folded or rolled up around various ingredients, mostly served with some sort of meat filling.

Pro Tip

The pancakes can be reheated in a steamer for about a minute when ready to serve. They also keep in the freezer for up to 3 weeks if you decide to make a larger batch.

INGREDIENTS

1 1/2 cups of all purpose flour
1/8 tsp salt
2/3 cup boiling water
1 teaspoon oil

INSTRUCTIONS

Mix the flour and salt in a heatproof bowl. Pour the boiling hot water into the flour mixture and use a spatula to mix until a dough ball forms. Once it is cool enough to handle, knead the dough for 8 minutes until smooth, adding flour if the dough is too sticky.

Cover with plastic and allow the dough to rest at room temperature for at least 1 hour.

Roll the dough into a cylinder and cut into 12 equal pieces. Form each piece into a ball, then flatten them out into a small disc about 2 inches in diameter. Lightly brush 6 of the discs with oil, ensuring the sides of the discs are also brushed with oil.

Layer the remaining 6 discs over the 6 oiled discs so you have 6 pieces, comprised of 2 discs each.

Use a rolling pin to roll the discs into 7-inch circles, flipping the pancakes frequently so both of the dough discs are rolled into the same size.

Heat a nonstick frying pan over medium low heat, and place one disc of two pancakes into the pan. After 30 to 45 seconds, you should see air pockets begin to form between the two pancakes. Flip the pancake; it should be white with just a couple of faint brown patches. Any more than that, and they are overcooked. After another 30 seconds, the air pockets should be large enough to separate the two pancakes.

Remove the pancakes to a plate, and let it cool for another 30 seconds. Now carefully pull apart the two pancakes at the seams. Place finished pancakes onto a plate and cover with a warm kitchen towel. Repeat until all pancakes are done.

Blackened Salmon with Mango Pico de Gallo

Blackened salmon is a succulent feast. Blackening gives fish a deep-black crust, without the burning or charring of conventional charbroiling. Topped with Pico de Gallo, or served over rice or with a salad, this blackened Salmon recipe is sure to become a firm favorite in no time.

Pro Tip

You want the pan to be extra hot so the fish blackens properly and doesn't stick. Use a heavy-bottomed, sturdy pan or cast iron skillet for the best results.

INGREDIENTS

3 salmon fillets (6oz each)
2 teaspoons paprika
1 teaspoon onion powder
1 teaspoon garlic powder
1 teaspoon oregano
1/2 teaspoon dried basil
1/2 teaspoon cayenne
1 teaspoon salt
1 teaspoon freshly cracked black pepper
1 tablespoon olive oil, divided
Pico de Gallo, for garnish

INSTRUCTIONS

To make the blackened salmon: Make a spice mix by combining all of the spice ingredients together (paprika, onion powder, garlic powder, oregano, basil, Cayenne, salt, pepper, olive oil).

Coat the salmon fillets with a small amount of oil. Generously sprinkle the fillets with the spice mix.

In a large skillet, heat 1 tablespoon of oil over medium heat. Once hot, add the salmon fillets and cook for about 3-4 minutes on medium heat depending on thickness, until crispy and blackened.

Flip the salmon fillets over and cook an additional 4-6 minutes. If your salmon fillets are browning too quickly, then turn down the heat.

Top with Mango Pico de Gallo (See recipe on page 60) and serve

Mango Pico de Gallo (for Blackned Salmon)

Pico de gallo´ (which literally means 'rooster's beak') is made from diced tomatoes, red onion, and chili pepper. this fresh and colorful salsa mexicana can either be served as a chunky salsa, or over any meat of fish.

INGREDIENTS

2 cups fresh mango
1 cup red onion
1 cup jicama
1/2 red bell pepper
1/2 green bell pepper
1 Serrano chile
1 jalapeño chile
1/4 cup cilantro
2 limes
1 tablespoon honey
1 teaspoon salt
1/2 teaspoon ground black pepper
1/2 teaspoon ground cumin
1/2 teaspoon garlic powder

INSTRUCTIONS

Peel and cut flesh of mango from pit. Dice into 1/4 inch cubes.

Peel skin from red onion. Dice into 1/4 inch cubes.
Peel skin from jicama. Dice into 1/4 inch cubes.

Trim end of each bell pepper, discard seeds and inner membrane. Dice into 1/4 inch cubes.

Trim stems off chiles and discard along with seeds. Dice into 1/4 inch cubes.

Trim cilantro leaves from stems and roughly chop.

In a medium sized bowl whisk together the lime juice, honey, salt, pepper, cumin and garlic powder.

Add all the mango, onion, jicama, bell peppers, chiles and cilantro to bowl. Toss to coat and refrigerate covered for 30 minutes minimum for flavors to meld.

 Season to taste.

Asian Lamb Lollipops

Marinated and seasoned Asian Lamb Lollipops are the perfect finishing touch for any meal. Pan seared to perfection these tender chops will become a staple in your household.

Pro Tip

Serving Suggestion:

This is a great dish for a large gathering, but you can easily adapt the recipe for fewer servings.

Serve these succulent lamb chops with some herbed couscous.

INGREDIENTS

1 pound (8-10) Lamb chops, frenched
1 cup brown sugar
1/2 tablespoon ground ginger
3 cloves garlic, minced
1/2 cup soy sauce
1 tablespoon chili garlic sauce
2 tablespoons olive oil
Cilantro, chopped for garnish
Green onion, chopped for garnish

INSTRUCTIONS

Whisk together in a bowl brown sugar, ground ginger, garlic, soy sauce, and chili garlic sauce. Place lamb chops in a resealable plastic bag and pour marinade over chops. Seal and massage ingredients together. Marinate in the fridge for 4-6 hours.

Using a large nonstick skillet or cast iron pan, heat oil over medium high heat. This may get a little smoky so turn on your fan.

Remove lamb chops from marinade, shake excess off. Sear in pan, each side about 2 minutes. Allow to rest.

Bring marinade to a rolling boil in a saucepan and reduce until thickened and syrup like consistency. Brush on chops after cooking.

Remove and garnish with chopped cilantro and green onion. Serve immediately.

Skirt Steak Plantain Tostadas

A simple marinade enlivens skirt steak for this Latin-inspired dish. Fried plantains are a delicious alternative to French fries.

INGREDIENTS

For the Tostones

4 green plantains, peeled and cut into 2-inch pieces
Vegetable oil for frying
Kosher salt, to taste

INSTRUCTIONS

To make the tostones: Fill a cast iron skillet with 1-inch of oil and heat to 375 degrees.

Place plantain pieces standing upright in oil and fry until light golden brown, about 3 minutes. Flip and fry second side for another 2 minutes. Remove to a paper towel lined platter and let sit until cool enough to handle.

Using an object with a flat bottom surface, smash the plantains to about 1/4" in height. Bring oil back to 375 degrees.

Working in batches, fry plantains until golden brown on each side, about 1 minutes per side. Remove to paper towel lined plate.

Season with salt

For the Toppings

1 small red onion, thinly sliced
Small red and orange sweet peppers, thinly sliced
1 medium jalapeño, thinly sliced
1/2 cup packed roughly chopped fresh cilantro leaves
1/2 cup sour cream
1/2 cup shredded cheddar cheese
Guacamole (optional)

INGREDIENTS

For the Steak

1 lb skirt steak
2 tablespoons vegetable oil
1 tablespoon Worcestershire sauce
2 teaspoons kosher salt
1 teaspoon brown sugar
1 teaspoon finely minced garlic (about 1 medium clove)
1/2 teaspoon ground cumin

INSTRUCTIONS

To make the steak: Whisk together oil, Worcestershire sauce, salt, brown sugar, garlic, and cumin in a small bowl. Place steak in a large resalable plastic bag and pour in marinade. Seal bag, removing as much air as possible, and place in refrigerator and let marinate 4 hours to overnight.

Heat 1 Tbsp. oil in a large skillet over medium-high. Cook steak until deeply browned, about 5 minutes per side for medium. Transfer to a cutting board; let sit 10 minutes before slicing.

Top tostadas with some guacamole (if desired) followed by steak, shredded lettuce, peppers, red onions, jalapeños, sour cream, shredded cheese and cilantro

Serve immediately.

SIDES

Sides

Crispy Smashed Potatoes — 67

Creamed Spinach — 69

Corn Souffle — 70

Sweet Fried Plantains — 71

Sweet Potato Mash w/ Brown Butter Sauce — 72

Roasted Veggies — 73

Chinese Bok Choy in Oyster Sauce — 75

Enoki Mushrooms w/ Garlic and Scallion Sauce — 76

Honey Garlic Butter Roasted Carrots — 77

Crispy Smashed Potatoes

The secret to these Crispy Smashed Potatoes comes from a very hot oven The surfaces of the potatoes become almost crusty under the intense heat, developing beautiful toastiness and crunch. Serve with your choice of meat and vegetables

Pro Tip

FOR CRISPIER POTATOES, bake until it is golden on the edges

INGREDIENTS

2 pounds small red, yellow or tri-color potatoes
1 tablespoon fine sea salt
3 tablespoons olive oil
1/4 teaspoon garlic powder
1/4 teaspoon onion powder
Freshly ground black pepper, to taste
2 tablespoons chopped fresh parsley, chives and/or green onion

INSTRUCTIONS

Preheat the oven to 425 degrees Fahrenheit.

To prepare the potatoes, scrub them clean if dirty and rinse under running water. Remove and discard any nubby sprouting areas. Place the potatoes in a large Dutch oven or soup pot.

Fill the pot with water until the potatoes are submerged and covered by 1 inch of water. Add 1 tablespoon of the salt. Bring the mixture to a boil over medium-high heat and continue cooking until the potatoes are very easily pierced through.

When the potatoes are done, drain them in a large colander and let them cool for about 5 minutes, until they can be handled safely.

Place them on a sheet pan and use a potato masher, a fork or a glass bottom container to gently smash each potato to a height of about 1/2 inch and place in a bowl.

Drizzle the olive oil over the smashed potatoes. Sprinkle the garlic powder, onion powder, salt and freshly ground black pepper over the potatoes.

Bake until slightly brown around the edges for about 15 to 20 minutes.

Sprinkle them with chopped fresh herbs and serve hot.

Creamed Spinach

Rich and creamy spinach is a delicious way to introduce more green vegetables into your diet and transform a simple appetizer or side dish.

INGREDIENTS

3 (10 oz) bags frozen chopped spinach
2 tablespoons butter
1 medium yellow onion, diced
6 large cloves garlic, minced
4 oz cream cheese
2 cups heavy cream
1 cup shredded mozzarella cheese
1/2 cup grated parmesan cheese
salt and pepper, to taste

INSTRUCTIONS

Defrost spinach in microwave or room temperature. Remove excess water (squeeze carefully using cheese cloth, a tea towel, or a colander) and set aside.

In a large skillet over medium high heat, melt butter. Add onion and sauté until translucent. Add garlic and cook for 30 seconds. Add the spinach and cook for 5 mins. Remove from the pan.

Add cream cheese to the empty pan and cook, stirring, until melted.

Add heavy cream and cook for 2 minutes. Add mozzarella cheese, parmesan cheese, salt and pepper. Stir till combined.

Fold in spinach into cream sauce and cook for an additional minute to reheat spinach

Corn Souffle

Corn soufflé is a common dish with many variations around the world that differ in style, presentation, ingredients, or all three. Some contain vinegar or other acidic ingredients to be more like "soupe aux maïs", while some use Mexican-style masa harina or Muffin mix to produce a lighter dish with distinct corn flavor

INGREDIENTS

1 (15 1/2 oz) can whole kernel corn, drained
1 (14 3/4 oz) can cream-style corn
1 (8 oz) pkg Jiffy Corn Muffin Mix
1 cup sour cream
1/2 cup butter, melted

INSTRUCTIONS

Preheat oven to 350

In a large bowl, combine the 2 cans corn, muffin mix, sour cream and melted butter.

Mix with a hand mixer and pour into a greased 9x13 casserole dish.

Bake for 35-45 minutes or until golden looking and a toothpick inserted comes out clean.

Sweet Fried Plantains

Plantains (not to be confused with bananas) are a delicious, versatile, and healthy treat that you should definitely be including in your diet. You can find them at most Latin American or Caribbean grocery stores or markets.

Pro Tip

The best plantains for this recipe are the ones that have very black skins and tender flesh. The darker they are the sweeter and less starchy which is what you want to get that deep caramelization

INGREDIENTS

4 large, very ripe plantains
1 1/2 cups vegetable oil
Kosher salt (optional)

INSTRUCTIONS

Trim ends of plantains, peel, and cut diagonally into 1" pieces.

Heat oil in a large skillet over medium-high.

Working in batches, cook plantains, turning once, until beginning to brown, 1–2 minutes per side.

Reduce heat to low and continue to cook, turning occasionally, until soft and deep golden brown, 6–8 minutes.

Transfer to a paper towel-lined sheet tray. Season with salt if desired.

Serve hot.

Sweet Potato Mash with Brown Butter Sauce

The Sweet Potato Mash is a creative and delicious way to take the familiar sweet potato and turn it in a whole new direction. Featuring a warm blend of butter, cream and brown sugar, that's sure to please the palate. This innovative recipe is one that everyone will love

INGREDIENTS

3 large sweet potatoes
1 stick of butter
2 tablespoons heavy cream
4oz softened cream cheese
1/2 cup of brown sugar
Sea salt and parsley, to garnish

INSTRUCTIONS

Preheat the oven to 350 degrees.

In a sauce pot, melt 1 stick of butter. Once the butter melts, allow it to continue cooking until it turns light brown, then turn off the heat and it will become browned butter.

Mix the heavy cream and cream cheese in a bowl until combined and set to the side.

Pierce each sweet potato with a fork and place on a baking sheet and cook for about 20 minutes or until they're fork tender.

When the potatoes are tender, remove the flesh from the skins and add them to a bowl. Using an electric mixer, whip the potatoes for about 2 minutes. This adds air to the potatoes and allows for the fibers to separate making them easily to discard.

Season the potatoes by adding in the browned butter, heavy cream mix, brown sugar, and then garnish with more butter and a bit of sea salt and parsley on top.

Roasted Veggies

Roasted Vegggies is a simple side dish that is great to serve with chicken, fish or pork. The cooking process in the oven is what brings out the sweetness of the vegetables. You can dress this side dish up or down with a variety of sauces from butter and parmesan cheese to an Asian-inspired sesame butter.

ROASTED RAINBOW CARROTS

INGREDIENTS

1lb rainbow carrots cut lengthwise in half
2 tablepoons olive oil
1 teaspoon Salt
1/2 teaspoon black pepper

INSTRUCTIONS

Preheat Oven to 400

Wash the carrots thoroughly and pat dry with a paper towel. Then spread them out on a baking sheet and drizzle with oil, sprinkle with salt, pepper then toss with your hands.

Roast the carrots for roughly 20 minutes, or until they're lightly caramelized around the edges and fork tender.

Pro Tip

You can dress these side dishes up or down with a variety of sauces from butter and parmesan cheese to an Asian-inspired sesame butter.

ROASTED BROCCOLINI

INGREDIENTS

2 bunches of broccolini
2 tablespoons olive oil
1 teaspoon Salt
1/2 teaspoon Black pepper

INSTRUCTIONS

Preheat Oven to 400

Trim 2 inches off the ends of the broccolini stems and discard, wash n pat dry. Cut any thick stalks in half lengthwise. Place the broccolini in a single layer on a sheet pan. (do not crowd the pan, the broccolini will steam rather than roast).

Drizzle sheet pan with 2 tablespoons olive oil, sprinkle with 1 teaspoon salt and 1/2 teaspoon pepper, and toss well.

Roast for 10 minutes, until the broccolini is crisp-tender. Sprinkle lightly with salt if needed.

ROASTED PARSNIPS

INGREDIENTS

1lb parsnips
2 tablespoon olive oil
1 teaspoon Salt
1/2 teaspoon black pepper

INSTRUCTIONS

Preheat Oven to 400

Wash parsnips and cut off ends and pat dry with a paper towel. Then spread them out on a baking sheet and drizzle with oil, sprinkle with salt, pepper then toss with your hands.

Roast the parsnips for roughly 20 minutes, or until they're lightly caramelized around the edges and fork tender.

Chinese Bok Choy in Oyster Sauce

EVERYDAY GOODNESS. A healthy dish with great favor, this Vegetable dish is a great side dish for a large or small group. It's seasoned with oyster sauce and sesame oil to ensure excellent quality in every bite.

INGREDIENTS

6 baby bok choy, clean and separate each leaf
2 tablespoons oyster sauce
1 tablespoon water
1 teaspoon sesame oil
1/2 teaspoon sugar
White pepper powder

Garlic Oil

2 cloves garlic, finely chopped
1 teaspoon oil

INSTRUCTIONS

Prepare the garlic oil first by heating up your wok and stir fry the minced garlic until they turn light brown. Dish out and set aside.

In a wok, heat up the sesame oil, and then add the oyster sauce, water, sugar, and white pepper powder.

As soon as the sauce heats up and blends well, drop your veggies into the wok and saute on high for 2 minutes.

As soon as they turn slightly wilted, transfer them to a platter. Top the vegetables with the garlic oil and serve immediately.

Enoki Mushrooms with Garlic & Scallion Sauce

This tender and tasty dish is quick and easy to prepare. These mushroms can be used over rice, ramen noodles or a baked potato. Great for a meatless dinner, add seared tofu or chicken for a heartier dish.

Pro Tip

Most vegetables take between 1-5 minutes. When the vegetables are done, quickly remove them from the boiling water with a slotted spoon and plunge them into the ice bath to stop the cooking process.

INGREDIENTS

14 ounces enoki mushroom
2 tablespoons oil
2 cloves minced garlic
3 tablespoons light soy sauce
1/2 teaspoon sugar
1/4 cup scallion finely chopped

INSTRUCTIONS

Be gentle when handling these enoki mushrooms. Trim away about 1-inch of the root section. Use your fingers to tear the enoki mushrooms into small bite size bundles and line them up neatly. Rinse clean and drain.

Prepare a wok with boiling water, and blanch the enoki mushrooms in two batches, cooking each batch for about 1 minute. Drain off the water and transfer the mushrooms to your serving plate.

In a small saucepan, heat the oil over medium heat. Add the garlic and cook for about 10 seconds (no need to brown the garlic).

Now add the light soy sauce, sugar, and scallions. Bring the sauce to a boil and turn off the heat. Don't overcook the garlic and scallions--we want that fresh and sweet taste!

Slowly pour the sauce over the enoki mushrooms and serve

Honey Garlic Butter Roasted Carrots

Tender and sweet, roasted carrots sing with the flavorful double-whammy of honey and garlic, and AN ALLTIME favorite: butter. This fast and easy vegetable dish pairs beautifully with poultry and beef dishes, but is also delicious all on its own

Pro Tip

PREPARE IN ADVANCE: You can peel and slice the carrots in advance. For maximum freshness, store them in a bowl of water in the refrigerator until you're ready to roast them. Drain and pat dry before proceeding

INGREDIENTS

1 pounds tri-color carrots or baby carrots
6 tablespoons unsalted butter
3 cloves minced or grated garlic
1 1/2 tablespoons honey
1 teaspoon salt
1/4 teaspoon freshly ground black pepper
2 tablespoons coarsely chopped fresh flat leaf parsley
Sea salt (optional)

INSTRUCTIONS

Arrange a rack in the middle of the oven and heat to 425°F.

Peel and trim the carrots. If they are more than 1-inch thick, cut them in half lengthwise; otherwise, leave them whole. Cut the carrots diagonally into 2-inch-long pieces. Place on a rimmed baking sheet; set aside.

Melt the butter in a small saucepan over medium heat. Continue cooking, swirling the pan occasionally, until the butter has a nutty aroma and is a golden-tan color, about 2 minutes. Add the garlic and continue to cook, swirling occasionally, until the butter is toasty-brown, about 30 seconds more. Remove from the heat, add the honey, and whisk to combine.

Drizzle half the brown butter sauce over the carrots and toss to coat. Sprinkle with the salt and pepper and toss to coat again. Spread the carrots into an even layer.

Roast 15 minutes. Flip the carrots, then roast until the carrots are tender and the edges are charred and crispy, about 15 minutes more.

Transfer to a serving bowl. Drizzle the remaining half of the brown butter sauce over the carrots, add the parsley, and toss to combine. Finish with a generous pinch of flaky sea salt, if using. Serve immediately.

SALADS & SALSAS

Salads & Salsas

Iceberg Wedge Salad	81
Mexican Street Corn Salad (Elote)	82
Greek Chickpeas Salad	83
Chilli Lime Shrimp Wrap	84
Peach, Tomato, and Corn, Arugula Salad	85
Cranberry Chicken Salad	86
Corn, Blackbean and Avocado Salsa	87
Spinach Salad	88

Iceberg Wedge Salad

THIS wedge salad is a classic accompaniment to any great steak dinner. Before you fire up the grill, make sure your guests are ready for mouthwatering flavor.

Pro Tip

Clean the lettuce after cutting into wedges if needed. This allows you to clean between all the layers of leaves. Be sure to do this step early to allow time for drying if needed.

INGREDIENTS

For the dressing- Ranch Dressing

1/2 cup mayonnaise
1/2 cup sour cream
1/2 cup buttermilk or regular milk
1/4 teaspoon onion powder
1/2 teaspoon garlic powder
1/4 teaspoon fine sea salt
1/8 teaspoon finely cracked pepper
freshly squeezed lemon juice to taste
approximately 1-3 teaspoons, adjust to taste

INSTRUCTIONS

Whisk together the mayo, sour cream and milk until smooth. Add the spices and whisk until combined. Add the lemon and whisk again.

Pour into a jar and chill in the refrigerator until ready to serve. This dressing will keep nicely in the refrigerator for up to a week. Enjoy!

INGREDIENTS

For the wedges salads-

1 iceberg lettuce cut into 4 (but we're only using 2)
1/3 cup bacon cooked and crumbled
4 hard boiled eggs chopped into pieces
10 grape tomatoes sliced in half
extra feta cheese crumbles 1-2 tablespoons per salad
chives for garnish

INSTRUCTIONS

In a small bowl, whisk all ingredients for the dressing together. Set aside.

On two dinner plates, place wedges of iceberg lettuce, cut side up.

Drizzle generously with dressing. Top with bacon, eggs, tomatoes, extra blue cheese and chives. Serve.

Mexican Street Corn Salad (Elote)

A great way to serve up some summertime fun!

Mexican street corn salad is the perfect dish to serve at your next picnic, bbq or party. This simple fresh corn salad recipe can be served warm, room temperature or chilled. Regardless of the occasion, it's sure to please your guests!

Pro Tip

Crema is like a Mexican sour cream and is found usually by the meat department with Hispanic items or the cheese. If you can't find it, you can substitute 1/4 cup sour cream and 1/3 cup mayonnaise.
Store in the refrigerator for up to 3 days.

INGREDIENTS

6 ears sweet corn, husked or fresh corn kernels
1/2 cup crema *see pro tip for substitution
4 tablespoons lime juice (fresh is best)
1/2 teaspoon ground cumin
3/4 teaspoon smoked paprika
1/2 teaspoon chili powder
1/4 teaspoon black pepper
1/4 teaspoon salt, plus more to taste
1/2 cup cheese crumbled cotija
1/2 onion red, minced
1/2 cup cilantro, chopped (optional)

INSTRUCTIONS

Heat a grill or cast iron skillet to medium heat. Add the corn or the kernels, turning occasionally until slightly charred on each side.

Remove from the grill and allow to cool for a few minutes.

Holding the corn by the small end, cut off all of the kernels.

Place the kernels in a big bowl and add all remaining ingredients.

Fold gently with a rubber spatula, seasoning with additional salt as needed.

Serve slightly warm, room temperature or cold.

Greek Chickpea Salad

Usually, when it comes to salads, chicken is the answer. But sometimes you want something lighter -- something meatless.
Here's a Greek-inspired chickpea dish that will satisfy meat eaters, vegetarians, or anyone in between.

Pro Tip

Serve the salad cold. Make an hour ahead if possible and store in the fridge.
Use avocado oil in place of olive oil if preferred.
Store in a container in the fridge for up to 5 days.

INGREDIENTS

1 15-ounce can chickpea (garbanzo, channa) rinsed and drained
1 English cucumber, halved and sliced into coins
2 cups halved cherry tomatoes
3/4 cup pitted kalamata olives, drained and halved
1/4 cup slivered red onion
6 ounces feta cheese, crumbled
1/3 cup extra virgin olive oil
2 tablespoons rice wine vinegar
1 teaspoon dried oregano
1 teaspoon kosher salt
1 teaspoon freshly ground black pepper

INSTRUCTIONS

In a large bowl, add the drained chickpeas, cucumber, tomatoes, kalamata olives, red onion, half of the feta cheese and oregano. Drizzle with the olive oil and vinegar then season with the kosher salt, freshly ground black pepper.

Toss gently and add the rest of the feta cheese. Adjust seasoning and serve or refrigerate overnight.

Chilli Lime Shrimp Wrap

These shrimp wraps are a perfect salad, light dinner or a great on-the-go appetizer that you can enjoy anywhere, even on the beach. The chili lime sauce is delicious and can be made with fresh or frozen shrimp

Pro Tip

Crisp up lettuce by soaking in ice water for a few minutes. Then, spin dry as you normally would. This is great for slightly wilted lettuce.

INGREDIENTS

1 lb. raw shrimp, peeled and deveined
2 teaspoons chili powder
1 teaspoon smoked paprika
2 cloves fresh garlic, minced
2 tablespoons extra-virgin olive oil, divided in half
2 teaspoons pink Himalayan salt
1 teaspoon freshly ground black pepper
1 lime
A handful of fresh cilantro leaves, chopped
2/3 cup Thai sweet Chili Sauce
8 romaine or butter lettuce leaves, rinsed and pat dried
1 large avocado, diced

INSTRUCTIONS

In a large glass bowl, add shrimp, all seasonings, juice of 1/2 lime, garlic, and 1 tablespoon of oil. Season with sea salt and pepper to your taste, then stir well to coat. Refrigerate/marinate for 30 minutes or more, covered.

Heat oil in a large skillet over medium heat. Add shrimp and cook until just pink, about 3 minutes
In a very large bowl add cooked shrimp, diced avocado, cilantro, chili sauce, juice of 1/2 lime and remaining oil.

Gently stir to combine.

Taste test and season with a pinch of sea salt and pepper of needed.
Add spoonfuls of the avocado shrimp mixture lettuce and enjoy.

Peach, Tomato & Corn Arugula Pasta Salad

Pasta is dressed to the nines with this one-of-a-kind salad. A zesty Dijon ,peaches. tomato and corn add freshness and color to earthy arugula in a pasta salad that's delightful—and nutritious.

INGREDIENTS

2-3 tablespoons extra virgin olive oil
1/2 cup Dijon Mustard
1/2 teaspoon sea salt, plus more to taste
freshly ground salt and pepper
1/4 teaspoon of red pepper flakes
4 ounces crumbled feta
2 large ripe peaches, sliced
1 pint cherry tomatoes, halved
1 cup thawed frozen corn or canned
1/2 medium red onion, thinly sliced
5 ounces bag baby arugula

INSTRUCTIONS

Bring a large pot of water to a boil and add a little salt. Once water boils, add the pasta and cook until al dente, about 7-9 minutes. Drain pasta, reserving a few tablespoons of water for later. Place pasta in large bowl.

In a small bowl, whisk together the olive oil, Dijon mustard, salt, pepper and red pepper flakes until well combined. Pour the dressing over warm pasta and add a little reserved pasta water to help keep the pasta moist and non-sticky. Immediately add feta and gently give the pasta a toss.

Next add in the peach slices, cherry tomatoes, corn, red onion and arugula. Toss to combine. Taste and add more of the dressing, salt and/or pepper, if necessary.

Cranberry Chicken Salad

Cranberry chicken salad is the best! It is always a favorite lunch, especially because it contains cranberries, which have been shown to have a number of health benefits.

In addition to the health benefits, this recipe also provides you with a savory meal that will get your brain thinking about what you need to do all afternoon without realizing it.

INGREDIENTS

2 chicken breasts, cooked and shredded
1/2 cup dried cranberries
1/2 cup chopped celery
1/2 cup finely chopped carrots
1/4 cup chopped pecans
1/4 cup mayonnaise
1/4 cup miracle whip
Salt
Black pepper

INSTRUCTIONS

Place shredded chicken in a mixing bowl along with the cranberries, celery, carrots and pecans and toss together

Blend in the mayonnaise and miracle whip to the chicken and mix well

Cover and refrigerate a few hours before serving

Serve with toasted baguette or assorted crackers

Corn, Black Bean & Avocado Salsa

This colorful bean and avocado salsa brings together the best of both worlds: Big, bold flavors and classic Mexican style. With fresh corn, black beans, and red onions, this salsa tastes like summer. And it's sure to be a hit at any tailgate or backyard BBQ!

INGREDIENTS

1 cup fresh corn kernels
1 can black beans (rinsed and drained)
1 avocado (diced)
1 tomato (diced)
1/4 cup diced red onion (diced)
1 tablespoon cilantro (chopped)
1 tablespoon lime juice (freshly squeezed)
Salt and pepper to taste

INSTRUCTIONS

Add the corn, black beans, avocado, tomato, red onion, cilantro, lime juice and salt and pepper in a bowl. Stir to combine. Taste and add lime and/or salt as needed

Spinach Salad

A healthy salad for all seasons, the perfect way to start a meal this Spinach Salad is a real crowd-pleaser. The blue cheese crumbles add a unique flavor to the dressing. This dish allows you to "eat your greens," even if you're not crazy about spinach! Bacon optional

Dressing

1/3 cup white balsamic vinegar
1/2 tablespoon of whole grain mustard
2 tablespoons honey
1/2 teaspoon Italian seasoning
salt and black pepper
3/4 cup of good olive oil

To make the dressing, add all of the ingredients except for the olive oil to a blender. Once all the ingredients have been added, turn the blender on low speed and then drizzle in the olive oil. Blend until well combined. Then, drizzle over the salad and enjoy.

INGREDIENTS

6-ounce bag of baby spinach
1 orange, peeled and separated
1/2 cup of pomegranate seeds
1/2 cup of crumbled blue cheese
1 1/2 cups of crumbled candy bacon

INSTRUCTIONS

Arrange all of the salad ingredients in a large bowl.

Candied Bacon

4 strips of thick cut bacon
1/2 cup of dark brown sugar
1 teaspoon of coarse ground black pepper

Preheat the oven to 350 degrees.
Lay out the slices of bacon on a baking rack and add a cookie sheet underneath to catch the drippings. Liberally season with brown sugar and cracked black pepper.

Roast the bacon in the oven for 15 minutes or until cooked through. Allow to rest for 3-4 minutes and it will harden as it cools.

DESSERTS

Desserts

Cheese Cake — 91

Guyanese Baked Custard — 94

Old Fashion Carrot Cake w/ Vanilla Cream Chese Frosting — 95

Blueberry Breakfast Cake — 97

Chocolate Mousse — 99

Cassava (Yuca) Pone — 101

Bread Pudding with Rum Sauce — 102

Cheesecake (Crust)

This treat requires no special skills and delivers impressive results. With simple ingredients, you can make perfectly creamy cheese cake that's superb on its own or topped with fruit.
It will be the star of any get together and is sure to be a hit with family and friends

INGREDIENTS

For one 9-inch Cake Crust:

1/3 cup sifted cake flour
3/4 teaspoon baking powder
Pinch of salt
3 large eggs, separated
1/3 cup sugar
1 teaspoon pure vanilla extract
2 drops pure lemon extract
2 tablespoons unsalted butter, melted
1/4 teaspoon cream of tartar

INSTRUCTIONS

Preheat the oven to 350°F and generously butter the bottom and sides of 9-inch springform pan (preferably a nonstick one). Wrap the outside with aluminum foil, covering the bottom and extending all the way up the sides.

In a small bowl, sift the flour, baking powder, and salt together.
Beat the egg yolks in a large bowl with an electric mixer on high for 3 minutes. With the mixer running, slowly add 2 tablespoons of the sugar and beat until thick light yellow ribbons form, about 5 minutes more. Beat in the extracts.

Sift the flour mixture over the batter and stir it in by hand, just until no more white flecks appear. Now, blend in the melted butter.

Now, wash the mixing bowl and beaters really well (if even a little fat is left, this can cause the egg whites not to whip). Put the egg whites and cream of tartar into the bowl and beat with the mixer on high until frothy.

Gradually add the remaining sugar and continue beating until stiff peaks form (the whites will stand up and look glossy, not dry).

Fold about one-third of the whites into the batter, then the remaining whites. Don't worry if you still see a few white specks, as they'll disappear during baking.

Gently spread out the batter over the bottom of the pan, and bake just until set and golden (not wet or sticky), about 10 minutes. Touch the cake gently in the center. If it springs back, it's done. Watch carefully and don't let the top brown.

Leave the crust in the pan and place on a wire rack to cool. Leave the oven on while you prepare the batter.

Watch the crust closely; since it's so thin, it needs only 10 to 12 minutes to bake

Cheesecake (Filling)

This treat requires no special skills and delivers impressive results. With simple ingredients, you can make perfectly creamy cheese cake that's superb on its own or topped with fruit. It will be the star of any get together and is sure to be a hit with family and friends

INGREDIENTS

For the Cream Cheese Filling:

4 (8 ounce) packages cream cheese
1 1/3 cups sugar
1/4 cup cornstarch
1 tablespoon vanilla extract
3 large eggs
1/4 cup heavy whipping cream

INSTRUCTIONS

Place one 8-ounce package of the cream cheese, 1/3 cup of the sugar, and the cornstarch in a large bowl.

Beat with an electric mixer on low until creamy, about 3 minutes, then beat in the remaining 3 packages of the cream cheese.

Increase the mixer speed to high and beat in the remaining 1 1/3 cups of the sugar, then beat in the vanilla.

Blend in the eggs, one at a time, beating the batter well after each one.

Blend in heavy cream.

At this point mix the filling only until completely blended. Be careful not to overmix the batter.

Gently spoon the cheese filling on top of the baked sponge cake layer.

Place the springform pan in a large shallow pan containing hot water that comes about 1 inch up the side of the pan.

Bake the cheesecake until the center barely jiggles when you shake the pan, about 1 hour 20 minutes.

Serve plain or with your choice of fresh fruit, or topping

Guyanese Baked Custard

There are desserts, and then there is a Guyanese baked custard. With the richness of a crème brûlée, it's that one dish guaranteed to satisfy any sweet tooth.

INGREDIENTS

6 large eggs
4 12oz cans of evaporation milk
1 cups sugar
2 tablespoons vanilla or almond extract (I used brown rum)
1 whole nutmeg

INSTRUCTIONS

Preheat the oven to 350 degrees

Blend up the eggs in a mixing bowl until fully combined

Add in all the remaining ingredients except for the nutmeg. Keep blending for about 5 minutes until sugar is completely dissolved and everything is mixed well together.

Pour out into a 9 x 13 baking dish or 12 - 4oz ramekins and grate the nutmeg over the entire top of the custard.

Place the dish in a hot water bath and put in the oven and bake for roughly 35-45 minutes.

Do not burn the top.

Old Fashioned Carrot Cake with Vanilla Cream Cheese Frosting

Our carrot cake is what the name implies, old fashioned. The real cream cheese frosting that tops this classic cake with layers of fluffy carrot cake stacked high with the fluffy frosting

Pro Tip

For the perfect texture, use the small holes of a box grater to grate your carrots. Thick chunks of carrots would not have time to thoroughly cook, especially when blended with flour, eggs, and other ingredients. Carrots serve to moisten the cake and add taste and texture, but not crunch

INGREDIENTS

2 cups of shredded carrots
2 cups sugar
1 1/2 cups vegetable oil
4 eggs
2 ½ cups of flour
2 teaspoons baking soda
2 teaspoons cinnamon
1 teaspoon salt
1/2 cup chopped pecans
3/4 cup raisins

For the frosting

1/2 cup of softened butter
12 oz softened cream cheese
1 vanilla bean
3 1/2 cups of confectioner's sugar

INSTRUCTIONS

Preheat oven to 350 degrees F.

Grease and flour a 9 x 13 or 2 - 8 inch baking pans. Add carrots, sugar, oil and eggs to a large bowl and beat well.

Mix flour, baking soda, cinnamon and salt and beat it into the carrot mixture. Stir in the pecans and raisins.

Bake for 30-40 minutes or util a toothpick inserted in the center comes out clean.

Cool cake in pan on a wire rack.

Prepare the frosting by combining the butter, cream cheese and vanilla in a bowl and beat util creamy. Add the confectioners' sugar to make the frosting a spreadable consistency.

Spread the frosting evenly over the cooled cake and sprinkle the top with some chopped pecans.

Blueberry Breakfast Cake

This delicious blueberry breakfast cake is baked on the outside yet soft and moist on the inside. It bursts with berry flavor and pairs amazingly well with fresh whip cream.

For the topping:

1/3 cup sugar
1/4 cup all-purpose flour
1 stick cold butter or margarine

For the drizzle:

Dark Chocolate Ganache
4oz dark chocolate or semi-sweet chocolate
1/2 cup heavy whipping cream

Heat cream on the stovetop until just simmering.

Turn off the heat and immediately pour cream over the chocolate and mix.

Let stand for 2 minutes and mix again until smooth.

Pro Tip

When heating cream for the drizzle DO NOT let it boil – it might cause the chocolate to split or go grainy.

INGREDIENTS

2 cups all-purpose flour
1/2 cup sugar
2 teaspoons baking powder
1 large egg lightly beaten
1/2 cup milk
1/4 cup butter or margarine softened (NOT melted)
1 teaspoon grated lemon peel
2 cups fresh or frozen blueberries

INSTRUCTIONS

Preheat the oven to 350 F and spray or grease a 9-inch square baking pan.

In a large bowl, whisk together flour, sugar and baking powder. Cut butter into small pieces. Add egg, milk, butter and lemon peel; mix just until dry ingredients are moistened. You may need to finish mixing with your hands to get all the flour incorporated. the batter will be very thick.

Fold in the blueberries. Because the batter is so thick, this may take a few minutes. Spread into a greased 9-in. square baking pan.

For topping, combine sugar and flour in a mini food processor or bowl. Add butter and process, or cut in if doing by hand, until mixture is crumbly. I like to do this with my fingers so I can tell when it's ready by touch. Sprinkle over batter

Bake at 350 degrees F for 40-45 minutes or until cake tests done.

Drizzle ganach lightly over the top of the cake and serve.

Chocolate Mousse

This is not your grandmother's chocolate mousse. This rich and creamy recipe is for the adventurous dessert lover who craves something more than the average, chocolatey and silky and not too-sweet mousse that will knock your socks off.

For Garnishes

1/3 cup heavy whipping cream, whipped to soft peaks and sweetened with 1 1/2 tablespoons of powdered sugar

Chocolate shavings and mint leaves for garnish

Pro Tip

The colder the cream, the easier it is to whip. Don't attempt to whip a low-fat cream. This is an impossible task because it has insufficient butterfat content.

INGREDIENTS

8 ounces semi-sweet chips (about 1 1/3 cups)
1/3 cup water
2 tablespoons unsweetened cocoa powder
1 tablespoon sugar
1/8 tsp salt
1 1/2 cups heavy whipping cream, whipped to stiff peaks
2 teaspoons vanilla extract
Mint leaves
Chocolate shavings

INSTRUCTIONS

Place the chocolate chips, water, cocoa, sugar, and salt in a large mixing bowl, and microwave in short, 30-second bursts, stirring after each interval, until the mixture is melted and smooth (this can also be done over a double boiler).

Fold in the whipped cream and vanilla extract.

Divide the mixture evenly between 6 dessert glasses, cover, and chill in the refrigerator until set (about 1 hour).

Top with sweetened whipped cream and sprinkle with chocolate shavings.

Cassava (Yuka) Pone

Made with grated cassave (yuka) this sticky and sweet Guyanese favourite dessert pairs nicely with any cold or hot beverage

INGREDIENTS

2 1/2 lbs grated cassava
8 oz freshly grated coconut
4 oz butter (softened)
2 oz lard
1 tablespoon vanilla extract
1 teaspoon nutmeg
1 teaspoon cinnamon powder
2 tablespoons grated ginger
1 cup raisins
2 cups brown sugar (sweetened to your liking)

INSTRUCTIONS

Preheat oven to 350 degrees F.

Prepare a 9 x13 baking dish, spray all sides.

Place all ingredients together in a large mixing bowl and mix using an electric hand mixer until combined.

Transfer to baking dish and bake for approximately 50 minutes or until golden brown.

Bread Pudding with Rum Sauce

If dessert is on your mind, pull up a seat at the table and let us introduce you to the deliciously rich bread pudding with rum sauce. Soaked in custard and baked to golden goodness and topped with decadent rum sauce. .

INGREDIENTS

1 loaf French bread, cut into 1 inch cubes (16 oz.)
4 cups milk
3 large eggs, beaten
2 cups sugar
1 cup raisin
3 tablespoons butter
2 tablespoons pure vanilla extract

For Rum Sauce

1/2 cup butter, softened
1 cup sugar
2 tablespoons Rum

Rum Sauce: Combine butter and sugar in a small saucepan; cook over medium, stirring frequently, until sugar dissolves.

Remove from heat, cool slightly; stir in bourbon.

INSTRUCTIONS

Combine bread and milk in a large mixing bowl; set aside for 5 minutes.

Add eggs, sugar, raisins, butter and vanilla; stir well.

Spoon mixture into a greased 3 quart casserole.

Bake, uncovered, at 325°F for 1 hour or until firm.

Cool in pan at least 20 minutes before serving.

Spoon into individual servings; serve with Rum Sauce.

DRINKS & COCKTAILS

Drinks & Cocktails

Mojito — 105

Caribbean Rum Punch — 106

Sorrel — 107

Ginger and Beet Juice — 108

Grapefruit Martini — 109

Mojito

Nothing says summer like a Mojito, a simple but delicious combo of rum, lime and soda water with sprigs of mint. This classic must have summer drink will be sure to please

INGREDIENTS

1/2 Lime cut into wedges
2 tablespoons sugar
8 fresh mint leaves
2 oz white rum
2 oz soda water
Ice

INSTRUCTIONS

Put the lime wedges, mint leaves and sugar into a tall glass and muddle them together, releasing the juice from the lime.

Fill the glass with ice. Add the rum and stir it all together.

Fill the glass with soda water. Enjoy.

Note

Increase or decrease the sugar to suit your taste
Sugar can be replaced with 2 tablespoons of simple syrup.

For the Simple Syrup

1/2 cup granulated sugar
1/2 cup water

Add the sugar and water to a small saucepan over medium heat.
Stir until sugar is dissolved.
Let cool, then pour into a glass jar and seal tightly with a lid.
Simple syrup will keep, refrigerated, for about one month

Caribbean Rum Punch

A tasty rum punch of finely aged Caribbean rums. A refreshing blend of light and gold rums blended with tropical fruits and citrus juices. Never watered down. Never too strong and that's what makes this recipe one for the ages!

INGREDIENTS

1/4 cup lime juice
1 cup orange juice
1 cup pineapple juice
1cup fruit punch
1 cup brown rum
1 cup coconut rum

INSTRUCTIONS

Stir all the ingredients together in a large pitcher or punch bowl.

Garnish with an orange and lime slices.

Serve over ice and enjoy

Sorrel Drink

A Christmas staple in Guyana but is drunk all year round. Refreshing, delicious and invorating, an excellent source of vitamin C, powerful antioxidant and anti-inflammatory properties, rich in compounds that can lower blood pressure, cholesterol and blood sugar levels.

INGREDIENTS

2 cups dried sorrel
24 oz water or (full a stock pot)
12 cloves
2 cinnamon sticks
2 cups of brown sugar (sweetened to your taste)

INSTRUCTIONS

Place the sorrel in a stainless steel pot along with the cloves and cinnamon sticks and add the water to full the pot.

Put on the pot to boil for about 15 to 20 minutes then turn the heat off.

Sweeten to taste with sugar

Leave to brew for at least 6 hours to overnight.

Strain well. Serve over ice.

Beet & Ginger Juice

Loaded with flavor, chock full of anti-oxidants, delicious and good for you

INGREDIENTS

2 small-medium red beets
4 large carrots
1 small Granny Smith apples
1 inch fresh ginger (skin removed)

INSTRUCTIONS

Gently rinse all juicing ingredients, especially if juicing the peels.

Cut beets and apples in wedges. Cut carrots in half or juice whole.

Juice all ingredients.

Mix juice as it will settle.

Pour fresh juice over ice to chill.

Grapefruit Martini

A delicious cocktail with a twist! This cold, refreshing martini can be made in minutes using ingredients found at your local liquor store. Its light taste is the perfect complement to any meal.

INGREDIENTS

2 ounces rum
1 1/2 ounces fresh grapefruit juice
1/2 ounce fresh lime juice
1/2 ounce agave
Dash or two of bitters (optional)

INSTRUCTIONS

Shake all ingredients in a cocktail shaker filled with ice.

Strain into a martini glass and garnish with fresh grapefruit slice..

RECIPE INDEX

GLOSSARY

APPENDIX

Recipe Index

AFRICAN
Creamed Spinach	69
Roasted Veggies	73
Honey Garlic Butter Roasted Carrots	77
Iceberg Wedge Salad	81

ASIAN
Vegetable Spring Rolls	31
Hoisin Beef	37
Punjabi Lamb Curry	45
Indian Rice Pilaf	49
Bibimbap	53
Roasted Duck Breast	55
Mandarin Pancakes	57
Asian Lamb Lollipops	61
Chinese Bok Choy in oyster Sauce	75
Enoki Mushrooms w/ Garlic and Scallion Sauce	76

CARIBBEAN
Pineapple Jerk Chicken Wings	23
Boil and Fried Cassava (Yuca)	51
Sweet Fried Plantains	71
Mojito	105
Caribbean Rum Punch	106
Sorrel	107

EUROPEAN
Salmon Cakes	11
Caprese Crostini	13
Charcuterie Board	15
Roasted Red Pepper Bisque	17
Prosciutto Crostini with Goat Cheese & Fig Jam	21
Chicken Gyros	47
Greek Chickpea Salad	83
Cheesecake	91
Blueberry Muffin Cake	97
Chocolate Mousse	99
Bread Pudding with Rum Sauce	102

GUYANESE
Black-eye Cookup Rice	41
Pepperpot (Indigenous)	43
Guyanese Baked Custard	91
Cassava (Yuca) Pone	101

MIDDLE EASTERN
Bacon & Cheese Cauliflower Rice Balls with Sriracha Dip	19
Spinach Salad	88
Ginger and Beet Juice	108

THE AMERICAS (NORTH, LATIN)
Shrimp Cerviche	25
Taco (Korean)	27
Crab Cakes (Indigenous)	29
Ribeye Steak & Grilled Shrimp	35
Butterflied Lemon Pepper Chicken	39
Blackened Salmon	58
Mango Pico de Gallo	60
Skirt Steak Plantain Tostadas	63
Crispy Smash Potatoes	67
Corn Souffle	70
Sweet Potato Mash w/ Brown Butter Sauce	72
Mexican Street Corn Salad (Elote)	82
Chili Lime Shrimp Wrap	84
Peach, Tomato, and Corn, Arugula Salad	85
Cranberry Chicken Salad	86
Corn, Black bean and Avocado Salad	87
Grapefruit Martini	109

Glossary

While some of these terms did not appear in this book, I have included it as a handy guide

A
A la carte (adj.) - separately priced items from a menu, not as part of a set meal.
Al dente (adj.) - cooked so it's still tough when bitten, often referring to pasta
A point (adj.) - cooking until the ideal degree of doneness, often referring to meat as medium rare
Acidulation (n.) - the process of making something acid or sour with lemon or lime juice
Aerate (v.) - the process when dry ingredients pass through a sifter and air is circulated through, changing the composition of the material, often referring to flour
Aspic (n.) - a dish in which ingredients are set into a gelatine made from a meat stock or consommé
Au gratin (adj.) - sprinkled with breadcrumbs and cheese, or both, and browned
Au jus (adj.) - with its own juices from cooking, often referring to steak or other meat
Au poivre (adj.) - coated with loosely cracked peppercorns and then cooked, often referring to steak

B
Bain Marie (n.) - a container holding hot water into which a pan is placed for slow cooking, otherwise known as a "water bath" or "double boiler"
Baste (v.) - to pour juices or melted fat over meat or other food while cooking to keep it moist
Bisque (n.) - a thick, creamy soup, with a base of strained broth (see coulis) of shellfish or game
Blanching (v.) - to plunge into boiling water, remove after moment, and then plunge into iced water to halt the cooking process, usually referring to vegetable or fruit
Braising (v.) - a combination-cooking method that first sears the food at high temperature, then finished it in a covered pot at low temperature while sitting in some amount of liquid
Brining (v.) - the process of soaking meat in a brine, or heavily salted water, before cooking, similar to marination

C
Chiffonade (n.) - shredded or finely cut vegetables and herbs, usually used as a garnish for soup
Consommé (n.) - a type of clear soup
Confit (n.) - meat cooked slowly in its own fat, usually referring to duck

Coring (v.) - to remove the central section of some fruits, which contain seeds and tougher material that is not usually eaten
Coulis (n.) - a thick sauce made with fruit or vegetable puree, used as a base or garnish
Croquette (n.) - a small round roll of minced meat, fish, or vegetable coated with egg and breadcrumbs

D
Deglaze (v.) - to remove and dissolve the browned food residue, or "glaze", from a pan to flavor sauces, soups, and gravies
Degrease (v.) - to remove the fat from the surface of a hot liquid such as a sauce, soup, or stew, also known as defatting or fat trimming
Dredging (v.) - to coat wet or moist foods with a dry ingredient before cooking to provide an even coating
Dress (v.) - to put oil, vinegar, salt, or other toppings on a salad or other food

E
Effiler (n.) - to remove the string from a string bean or to thinly slice almonds

F
Fillet (n.) - a boneless piece of meat, poultry, or fish; the French version, spelled as "filet," is also used when referencing a cut of beef that is boneless, such as filet mignon
Flambe (v.) - the process of adding alcohol such as brandy, cognac, or rum to a hot pan to create a burst of flames
Frenching (v.) - the process of removing all fat, meat, and cartilage from rib bones on a rack roast by cutting between the bones with a sharp paring knife, often referring to lamb, beef, or pork rib

G
Galette (n.) - flat, round cakes of pastry, often topped with fruit or a food prepared in served in the shape of a flat round cake, such as "a galette of potatoes"
Gazpacho (n.) - a Spanish dish of cold, uncooked soup, which typically contain tomatoes, cucumbers, onions, garlic, oil, and vinegar

H
Harissa (n.) - a spicy, aromatic chile paste made from a variety of hot peppers and spices, often used in North African and Middle Eastern cooking

I
Infusion (n.) - the process of extracting chemical compounds or flavors from a vegetable in water, oil, or alcohol, by allowing the material to remain suspended in the liquid over time, also known as steeping
Isinglass (n.) - a pure, transparent form of gelatin, obtained from the bladders of certain fish, used in jellies as a clarifying agent

J
Jacquarding (v.) - the process of poking holes into the muscle of meat in order to tenderize it, also known as needling
Jeroboam (n.) - an oversize wine bottle holding about three liters
Jus lie (n.) - meat juice that has been lightly thickened with either arrowroot or cornstarch

K
Kipper (n.) - a whole herring that has been split into a butterfly fashion from tail to head, gutted, salted, or pickled
Kirsch (n.) - a fragrant, colorless, unaged brandy distilled from fermented cherries, used with fondue
Kissing Crust (n.) - the portion of an upper crust of a loaf of bread which has touched another loaf when baking

L
Lactobacillus (n.) - a bacterium usually found in fermenting products, such as yogurts
Larding (v.) - the process of inserting strips of fat into a piece of meat that doesn't have as much fat, to melt and keep the meat from drying out
Liaison (v.) - a binding agent of cream and egg yolks used to thicken soups or sauces

M
Macerate (v.) - the process of softening or breaking into pieces using liquid, often referring to fruit or vegetables, in order to absorb the flavor of the liquid
Marinate (v.) - the process of soaking foods in seasoned and acidic liquid before cooking for hours or days, adding flavor to the food
Mignonette (n.) - roughly cracked or coarsely ground peppercorns, used for au poivre dishes or for mignonette sauce, which contains vinegar and shallots as well and is often used for oysters

Mince (v.) - to finely divide food into uniform pieces smaller than diced or chopped foods, prepared using a chef's knife or food processor

Mise en place (v.) -the preparation of ingredients, such as dicing onions or measuring spices, before starting cooking
Mother (n.) - the base sauce used to make other variations of the original sauce; there are five variations: brown or espagnole, velouté, béchamel, tomato sauce, and emulsions

N
Nappe (n.) - the ability of a liquid to coat the back of a spoon or the act of coating a food, such as a leg of lamb, with glaze
Needling (v.) - injecting fat or flavors into an ingredient to enhance its flavor

O
Ort (n.) - a scrap or morsel of food left over after a meal
Ouzo (n.) - an anise-flavored, strong, colorless liquor from Greece

P
Parboiling (v.) - the process of adding foods to boiling waters, cooking until they are softened, then removing before they are fully cooked, usually to partially cook an item which will then be cooked another way
Parcooking (v.) - the process of not fully cooking food, so that it can be finished or reheated later
Pâté (n.) - a mixture of seasoned ground meat and fat minced into a spreadable paste
Polenta (n.) - a mush or porridge made from yellow or cornmeal which originated in Northern Italy
Praline (n.) - a confection of nuts cooked in boiling sugar until brown and crisp

Q
Quadriller (v.) - to make criss-cross lines on the surface of food, as part of food presentation
Quatre-epices (n.) - literally meaning "four spices," a finely ground mixture of generally pepper, cinnamon, nutmeg, ginger, or cloves, used to season vegetables, soups, and stews

R
Remouillage (n.) - a stock made from bones that have already been used once to make a stock, making it weaker
Render (v.) - to cook the fat out of something, such as bacon

S
Sautéing (v.) - to cook food quickly over relatively high heat, literally meaning "to jump" as the food does when placed in a hot pan
Scald (v.) - to heat a liquid so it's right about to reach the boiling point, where bubbles start to appear around the edges

Sear (v.) - a technique used in grilling, baking, or sautéing in which the surface of the food is cooked at high temperature until a crust forms
Soupe aux mais (n) – A soup made of corn
Steep (v.) - to allow dry ingredients to soak in a liquid until the liquid takes on its flavor, often referring to coffee, tea, or spices
Sweat (v.) - gently heating vegetables in a little oil, with frequent stirring and turning to ensure emitted liquid will evaporate; usually results in tender, or in some cases such as onions', translucent pieces

T
Tempering (v.) - raising the temperature of a cold or room-temperature ingredient by slowly adding hot or boiling liquid, often referring to eggs
Trussing (v.) - to tie meat or poultry, such as turkey with a string, woven through the bird parts by using a needle, in order to create a more compact shape before cooking

U
Ultra-pasteurization (n.) - the process of heating up milk products to 280 degrees Fahrenheit for a few seconds and chilling it down rapidly, resulting in milk that's 99.9% free from bacteria and extending their shelf-life
Unleavened (adj.) - made without yeast or any other leavening agent, often referring to bread

V
Vandyke (v.) - to cut a zig-zag pattern around the circumference of a lemon to create decorative garnishes for food presentation
Vol-au-Vent (n.) - a round pastry that is baked and then filled with meat or vegetables after the fact

W
Whip (v.) - to beat food with a mixer to incorporate air and produce volume, often used to create heavy or whipping cream, salad dressings, or sauces
Whisk (n.) - a cooking utensil used to blend ingredients in a process such as whipping

X
Xanthan gum (n.) - a food additive, commonly used to thicken salad dressings, that is water-soluble and produced by the fermentation of sugar with certain microorganisms
Xylitol (n.) - a naturally fulfilling alcohol found in most plants such as fruits and vegetables, widely used as a sugar substitute in sugar-free chewing gums, mints, and other candies

Y
Yakitori (n.) - a Japanese dish of small pieces of boneless chicken that is marinated, skewered, and grilled

Z
Zest (v.) - to cut the zest, or the colorful part of the skin that contains oils and provide aroma and flavor, away from the fruit

Appendix

BASIC KITCHEN CONVERSIONS & EQUIVALENTS

DRY MEASUREMENTS CONVERSION CHART
3 TEASPOONS = 1 TABLESPOON = 1/16 CUP
6 TEASPOONS = 2 TABLESPOONS = 1/8 CUP
12 TEASPOONS = 4 TABLESPOONS = ¼ CUP
24 TEASPOONS = 8 TABLESPOONS = ½ CUP
36 TEASPOONS = 12 TABLESPOONS = ¾ CUP
48 TEASPOONS = 16 TABLESPOONS = 1 CUP

LIQUID MEASUREMENTS CONVERSION CHART
8 FLUID OUNCES = 1 CUP = ½ PINT = ¼ QUART
16 FLUID OUNCES = 2 CUPS = 1 PINT = ½ QUART
32 FLUID OUNCES = 4 CUPS = 2 PINTS = 1 QUART = ¼ GALLON

128 FLUID OUNCES = 16 CUPS = 8 PINTS = 4 QUARTS = 1 GALLON

1 CUP = ¼ QUART
1 CUP = 1/16 GALLON
1 CUP = 240 ML
1 MILLILITER = 1/5 TEASPOON
5 ML = 1 TEASPOON
15 ML = 1 TABLESPOON
240 ML = 1 CUP OR 8 FLUID OUNCES
1 LITER = 34 FL.

WEIGHT
1 CUP BUTTER = 2 STICKS = 8 OUNCES = 230 GRAMS = 8 TABLESPOONS

1 CUP ALL-PURPOSE FLOUR = 4.5 OZ
1 CUP ROLLED OATS = 3 OZ
1 LARGE EGG = 1.7 OZ
1 CUP BUTTER = 8 OZ
1 CUP MILK = 8 OZ
1 CUP HEAVY CREAM = 8.4 OZ
1 CUP GRANULATED SUGAR = 7.1 OZ
1 CUP PACKED BROWN SUGAR = 7.75 OZ
1 CUP VEGETABLE OIL = 7.7 OZ
1 CUP UNSIFTED POWDERED SUGAR = 4.4 OZ

OVEN TEMPERATURES
120 C = 250 F
160 C = 320 F
180 C = 350 F
205 C = 400 F
220 C = 425 F

BAKING PAN CONVERSIONS
9-INCH ROUND CAKE PAN = 12 CUPS
10-INCH TUBE PAN = 16 CUPS
10-INCH BUNDT PAN = 12 CUPS
9-INCH SPRINGFORM PAN = 10 CUPS
9 X 5 INCH LOAF PAN = 8 CUPS
9-INCH SQUARE PAN = 8 CUPS

BAKING IN GRAMS
1 CUP FLOUR = 140 GRAMS
1 CUP SUGAR = 150 GRAMS
1 CUP POWDERED SUGAR = 160 GRAMS
1 CUP HEAVY CREAM = 235 GRAMS

1 GRAM = .035 OUNCES
100 GRAMS = 3.5 OUNCES
500 GRAMS = 1.1 POUNDS
1 KILOGRAM = 35 OUNCES

www.ingramcontent.com/pod-product-compliance
Lightning Source LLC
Chambersburg PA
CBRC091212010526
44119CB00021B/378